Pictures Past

A CENTENNIAL CELEBRATION
OF
UTAH STATE UNIVERSITY

by

A. J. Simmonds

1988
UTAH STATE UNIVERSITY PRESS
LOGAN, UTAH

Library of Congress Cataloging-in-Publication Data

Simmonds, A. J.
    Pictures past.

    1. Utah State University–History. I. Utah
State University. II. Title.
LD5515.S56 1988 378.792'12 87-34623
ISBN 0-87421-134-4

Grateful acknowledgment is made to Utah State University Special Collections and Archives for the use of historical photographs, to the contributors and donors to the collections, and to the fine work of University Photographer Ted Hansen. The photograph of the Space Shuttle was used with permission from the National Aeronautics and Space Administration (NASA).

The paper used in this publication is Warren Cameo Dull 80 lb. and meets the minimum requirements of the American National Standard for Permanence of Paper for Printed Library Materials, Z39.48 - 1984.

Table of Contents

First student body and faculty photograph, Spring, 1891.

Show me a Scotsman . . .

Show me a Scotsman who doesn't love the thistle;
Show me an Englishman who doesn't love the rose;
Show me a true-hearted Aggie from Utah
Who doesn't love the spot where the sagebrush grows.

Those are the words—no longer much known even by those who know the tune (regularly played at USU home games)—to the Aggie Fight Song, a song that dates from at least the turn of the century. That is fitting, since this book records another turn of the century, the Centennial of Utah State University.

In the following pages, the terminology tends to reflect current usage—even though that practice is historically awkward. For example, the term Taggart Student Center is exclusively used for what was known from 1952 to 1968 as the Union Building. Likewise, the Ray B. West Building is used for that structure, built in 1919 and later known as Engineering, then as Education.

In the case of the name of the institution itself, I have tried to be historically accurate and use the correct name as the institution grew and evolved from a college to a university. Since its founding on March 8, 1888, the University has had four official names:

    Agricultural College of Utah, 1888-1916
    Utah Agricultural College, 1916-29
    Utah State Agricultural College, 1929-57
    Utah State University, 1957-

This book does not pretend to present a comprehensive history of Utah State University. It cannot. It presents glimpses of that institution, glimpses that can be documented by the photographs preserved in University Archives. Entire areas of the University's past are ignored for no better reason than that no one had an available camera to record them; or that, once recorded, they never found their way into University Archives.

The entire story is not told. That is the responsibility of another. I leave it to him.

And if these pages are much concerned with the early years when the institution was new, I can only plead that there is where the author's interests are also centered—when the land was new and when beginnings were made.

This is my book.

That must be clearly said, lest others receive opprobrium for the choices and conclusions that are mine alone. Thanks are due to those who tolerated my intolerable delays in producing it and to one who has helped in minimizing the delays and enriching the result: Jeannie.

This is my book. It is dedicated to the memory of Andrew Charles Simmonds, I, 1872-1947, who enrolled at Utah State on January 5, 1892—and who wouldn't have believed what's happened since.

A. J. Simmonds,
Curator, Special Collections,
Utah State University

C.L. Thompson's plan for "The College Building" was for a much smaller Old Main, with the tower centered directly on the east end of Fifth North Street.

CHAPTER ONE

The Beginnings

Utah State University's legal and institutional beginnings can be traced back to the mid-nineteenth century. President Abraham Lincoln signed the Morrill Act on July 2, 1862, which provided for a grant of land from the federal government to the several states and territories of 30,000 acres of the public domain for each representative and senator. The subsequent sale of the land would provide an endowment to establish colleges that would, in the words of the act, support and maintain institutions

> where the leading object shall be, without excluding other scientific and classical studies, and including military tactics, to teach such branches of learning as are related to agriculture and the mechanic arts, in such manner as the Legislatures of the States may respectively prescribe, in order to promote the liberal education of the industrial classes in the several pursuits and professions of life.

The Territory of Utah did not take advantage of the congressional act until 1888, when the Utah Legislative Assembly passed a bill sponsored by Representative Anthon H. Lund. The Lund Act, signed by territorial Governor Caleb West on March 8, 1888, was the result of considerable behind-the-scenes maneuvering by the Cache County delegation to the assembly and its political allies. Although the entire assembly agreed that Utah should take advantage of the Land-Grant Act and establish an agricultural college (the bill was to pass unanimously), there was considerable polit-ical horse trading to secure the institution for Cache County. Other territorial institutions had already been established. The capital and the University of Utah were in Salt Lake County and the Territorial Insane Asylum in Utah County. Two additional institutions were to be established by action of the 1888 assembly: the Land-Grant College and the Reform School. The college bill carried an appropriation of $25,000 and the reform school bill one of $75,000. Weber County chose the larger appropriation; and Cache County got the College!

By law, the first Board of Trustees consisted of the territorial Governor, the Secretary, and the County Assessors of Cache, Davis, Salt Lake, Sanpete, and Utah counties. John T. Caine, Jr., of Logan was chosen Secretary of the College—a position he held for over thirty years. The Trustees' first year was spent selecting a site for the College. A joint committee of the Logan City Council and the Cache County Court (territorial predecessor of the County Council) met throughout 1888 to choose a campus site. In September, the Trustees recommended the purchase of a seventy-five-acre farm in Providence for $3,000, with the city paying $1,000 and the county $2,000. County Judge William Goodwin would not hear of that arrangement. According to Goodwin, it would be fifty-fifty, or the county would not participate. The committee went back to work with instructions from Judge Goodwin to find a cheaper campus. Three other sites in Providence and one in Hyrum were

The Honorable William Goodwin was Cache County Judge in 1888. He found property in Logan that could be acquired cheaply, and overruled the placement of the College in Providence.

In 1889, territorial Governor Caleb W. West chose the location where Old Main stands today.

investigated, with the final recommendation being for an eighty-five-acre site, again in Providence, for $5,000. The City Council agreed to pay one half; but Judge Goodwin thought it far too expensive.

Little thought was given to placing the College in Logan. Logan already boasted the LDS church-owned Brigham Young College, and many citizens believed that better agricultural sites could be located outside of the city. Then, on February 6, 1889, Judge Goodwin found a bargain. Zions Savings Bank & Trust foreclosed on the property of the Logan, Hyde Park, and Smithfield Canal Company and sold the company's property at auction—including a 100-acre site on the Logan bench. The canal company, however, held an option to buy back the 100 acres. This was Judge Goodwin's bargain. The joint committee bought the 100 acres for $2,500 and deeded back forty- five acres to the company, and had fifty-five acres left over for a campus—the heart of the present campus. Succeeding generations must admit that Judge Goodwin, whatever his motives—picked

a winning site. The final purchase was made on April 1, 1889. However, a year later, in auditing county expenditures, Judge Goodwin discovered that the County had overpaid its half by $78.73—and promptly billed the city for that amount!

Even without a secured site, the Board of Trustees had advertised for plans for "The College Building" (later known as Old Main) and only two weeks after the campus was secured, it met in Logan and chose the plans submitted by C. L. Thompson that called for a three-part building ultimately measuring 100 by 270 feet. The Board decided that the south wing of the building in Thompson's plan should be built immediately. The next day, April 16, 1889, Board members walked over the site of the future campus, and Caleb W. West, territorial Governor and ex-officio President of the Board, chose the spot where the structure would be built. The Governor picked the location so that the tower of the completed building would be located due east of the end of Logan's Seventh Street—today's Fifth North.

West's successor, territorial Governor Arthur L. Thomas, laid the cornerstone.

Teams of horses hauling a boiler for Old Main from the Logan depot. The photo, circa 1910, shows the intersection of Main and Center Streets with the Thatcher Opera House in the background.

The only structure on campus specifically built as a home was for the Director of the Experiment Station (whom it was assumed would also be the President of the Agricultural College of Utah). Moved to accommodate the building of Smart Gym in 1912, the house had several campus locations until it was torn down in 1968.

After advertising for bids in all the leading papers in Utah Territory, on May 18, 1889, the Board awarded the construction contract to Sommer, Peterson & Company of Logan for a low bid of $20,305. The company started work immediately, and on July 27, 1889, the new territorial Governor, Arthur L. Thomas, laid the cornerstone to appropriate music provided by the Logan Firemen's Brass Band. Work progressed rapidly, and the first phase of Old Main was completed and accepted by the Trustees on February 22, 1890.

That same month, the territorial assembly appropriated $48,000 to provide additional buildings and equipment for the College and the Agricultural Experiment Station, and during the summer of 1890 the President's House, the Experiment Station Director's House, the Model Barn, the Experiment Station Building, and the beginnings of the College Boarding House were built.

Meanwhile, the first staff was assembled. The key appointment was perceived as the Director of the Agricultural Experiment Station, and the job of finding the first

The Model Barn was built in 1890 as a laboratory for the agricultural programs of the College.

Director was given to Secretary John T. Caine, Jr., the only individual on the Board (and probably the only one in Utah) who had formally studied agriculture at an eastern college: Cornell. Writing to one of his former professors, I. P. Roberts, Caine elicited several names, among them Jeremiah Wilson Sanborn of the University of Missouri, a man who had published extensively on scientific agriculture.

Caine wrote to Sanborn and offered him the $2,500 salary authorized by the Board of Trustees. Sanborn turned it down. Feeling strongly that the new Utah Agricultural Experiment Station needed the stature and firm start that Sanborn could provide, Caine wrote a long, detailed personal letter to him outlining the Utah situation, the new institution, and the condition of Logan and Cache Valley. The letter, plus more money, worked. Sanborn agreed to come for a salary of $3,000 a year and a suite of living quarters in Old Main. The Board agreed, and on January 20, 1890, Jeremiah W. Sanborn, the first of the academic community to come to Utah State University, stepped from the train at the Logan depot.

Dr. Jeremiah Wilson Sanborn, first President of the Agricultural College of Utah, 1890-94.

Sanborn lived with the Caines for five months, during which time he established the basic program of the Experiment Station and recommended most of the staff. He so impressed the Board of Trustees, that on May 17, 1890, it gave him additional responsibility, electing him President of the Agricultural College of Utah.

The College was formally dedicated on September 4, 1890, and opened the next morning for instruction. There were some changes. The house designed by Sanborn as a model farmhouse for the teaching of domestic science was taken over by the President as his official residence. He "traded" the Domestic Science Department the five rooms in the south wing of Old Main that he was to have had as an apartment.

The President's House was built as a model farmhouse. Initial plans called for it to be the home of the School of Domestic Science, but President Sanborn moved in as soon as it was completed.

The College began with a faculty of nine – some of whom also worked in the research program of the Agricultural Experiment Station. One program that Sanborn instituted, and that remained a fixture until 1904, was the Preparatory Department – under the redoubtable John T. Caine, Jr. Essentially, it was a high school, and Sanborn explained its purpose in the College's first publication.

> The state of development of our public schools seems to require, for a few years, a preparatory department of one year for the fitting of those students who are unable to pass an examination for entrance to the college courses. This, it is hoped, will be a temporary necessity.

The Boarding House, the first dormitory, was completed in 1891. It housed both men and women – and a very watchful matron! Houses for workers on the Experiment Station farm were built, and the first experiment plots were staked out northwest of Old Main in the area now occupied by the Taggart Student Center and the University Inn. Sanborn reported that during 1890-91 the College enrolled 139 students, 106 men and 33 women, and that spring he posed with them and the faculty in the first group picture taken at what everyone in the Territory of Utah was calling the "AC."

Right:
Mrs. Sarah Godwin Brown Goodwin was the first librarian. This photo shows her among Library stacks in the early 1900s, when the Library was housed in Old Main.

The entire campus of the Agricultural College of Utah in the spring of 1902 with the tower partially completed. Note the multiple privies behind the dormitory.

The campus from the intersection of Sixth East and Fifth North about 1899.

CHAPTER TWO

College Town

In the 1890s a special edition of the *Journal* referred to Logan as "The Athens of Utah." That may have been a bit exaggerated, but not much, for in 1892 Logan was the home of not one but two colleges: the Agricultural College of Utah and the Brigham Young College. In addition, the town boasted a public high school; a private high school (the New Jersey Academy); two private grammar schools (Trinity and St. John's); and five public schools. That is quite a record for a city only thirty-three years old and with only 4,700 people, highlighting the area's historical concern for education.

Logan was founded in May 1859 and by 1862 was the largest city, as well as the County Seat of Cache County. Although Logan was originally an agricultural settlement, the Logan River provided enough water power that by 1875 the city had several industries and the first high school in Utah outside of Salt Lake City. Two years later the Mormon Church established the Brigham Young College, an institution of secondary and higher education that, until it closed in 1926, provided the chief rivalry to Utah State University. With two colleges in the same town, it could not have been otherwise.

The Logan business district initially developed at the intersection of Main and First North where the Cache Stake Tithing Office, the valley's major economic center, was located behind cobblestone walls. When the railroad reached Logan in 1873, the focus shifted to Center Street,

which connected the downtown with the depot of the Utah & Northern Railroad; and it was just off Center, at First South and First West, where the Brigham Young College was located after 1885.

The construction of the Logan LDS Temple between 1877 and 1884 altered the focus of the city from Main Street toward the East Bench, but it was the location of the Agricultural College of Utah on the high bench in 1889 that permanently altered the city. Rather than follow the previous developments to the north and southwest that had occurred because of irrigation and road systems, the newer development moved the city northeast onto the benches.

The College formed an almost separate village away from Logan proper. Surviving letters from President Joshua H. Paul, the second President of the College, indicate that the President kept a buggy in the Model Barn and tried to get downtown at least once a week! Because the College was out of the city, mobility presented a problem. When the members of the legislature visited the College in the winter of 1904 (Utah was admitted to the Union as the 45th State on January 4, 1896), they were met at the Logan depot by a line of borrowed carriages and carried to campus in a procession that stretched out for a quarter of a mile and took half an hour.

The first real measure to physically unite Town and Gown came in 1909 when the College closed its Boarding House, forcing all students to rent quarters in downtown

The Brigham Young College, operated by the LDS Church from 1877 to 1926, was in downtown Logan

The East Building of Brigham Young College, circa 1888, showing some of the students who constituted ACU's biggest rivals.

The first known photograph of Logan was taken in May 1884, at the time of the dedication of the Logan Temple.

The bench where USU would be started six years later shows no building or development.

Main Street, Logan, 1895, the year after the College graduated its first class.

Logan. New homes built northwest of the Temple were often built with separate apartments that could be rented to the students. In 1912 the campus and the downtown were firmly connected by the tracks of the Logan Rapid Transit Company, a trolley line that formed part of the Utah-Idaho Central Railroad, an electric passenger line that connected Preston, Idaho, with Ogden, Utah.

With ready communication either by streetcar or by automobile in the years after 1910, the College was firmly integrated into Logan City and many campus events were scheduled for downtown locations. For example, student operas and plays moved from Old Main to the stage of the Thatcher Opera House at Main and Center. They had to move back again after the Opera House burned in April 1912. (The fire also destroyed the costumes and scenery for the College production of "The Mikado.")

When the Brigham Young College closed in 1926, many of its students transferred to the Agricultural College, but even more telling was that the AC was now the sole focal point for higher education in the city and a base for a growing number of students and faculty. Business firms that had originally ended at Second North and Main started

Joshua H. Paul, second President of the Agricultural College of Utah, 1894-96.

Downtown Logan in 1902, looking over the rooftops toward the campus.

The first faculty of the Agricultural College of Utah.

Transporting crowds from downtown to the campus called for many buggies, surries, and carriages, as this photo showing the visit of the state legislature, circa 1901, illustrates.

to relocate further north on Main Street and thus closer to the College. It was a development that continued and was accelerated by the first housing development on the bench near the College, the Morningside Park development following World War II. During the 1950s, the College began to build dormitories on campus and USU became a resi-

dence campus. Numerous private apartment complexes were built adjacent to the campus on the west and the community also moved north.

Until the early 1960s, Fifth North and the Boulevard provided the most usual means of communication between the city and the campus. With the widening of Fourth North

The Logan Republican.

The proof of the value of Republican advertising lies in the healthy returns given to its advertisers.

If you want all the news; take The Republican—30c a month in Logan; 25c a month in Cache county.

EIGHT PAGES   LOGAN, CACHE COUNTY UTAH, THURSDAY, SEPTEMBER 12, 1912.   TENTH YEAR

TOLL OF COLLEGE BELLS TO SOUND O'ER LOGAN "THE ATHENS OF THE WEST"

The Agricultural College's reputation was growing: by 1912 the "Athens of Utah" had become the "Athens of the West."

Right:
The brass band of the Agricultural College of Utah leads the parade down Main Street on Logan's fiftieth anniversary of settlement on May 6, 1909.

Logan's South Main Street in 1919, showing the tracks of the Logan Rapid Transit Company, the electric trolley line that connected the campus with the city.

to four lanes and the remaking of Fourth North as the main road into Logan Canyon (replacing Canyon Road), the main entry to the campus moved from the north and west sides to the south and east sides, and the intersection of Fourth North and Main Streets changed from a residential to a business section at least partially oriented to the growing community centered on the University campus. By the mid-1970s, the city had moved along Main Street all the way to Fourteenth North, where a mall and shopping center were built. More apartments were built north and west of campus, so the entrance to campus along Eighth East is now also very busy. The campus has become a vital part of the community.

The Logan Island, circa 1949. Originally a thicket of willows and cottonwoods, it became farmland in the 1870s. Today it is a developed housing area.

Northwest Logan from College Hill, circa 1949.

Logan and the Logan Temple in 1978, photographed from the Utah State University campus.

Fourth North Street became the major artery connecting the campus and the town in the 1960s. This 1975 photo shows the business development along the street.

In 1891, at the close of its first year of operation, the College's student body and staff constituted a bare one-quarter of one percent of the city's population. In 1986 that same group constituted one-third of the people in Logan; and their dependents increased that percentage. It would be false, however, to indicate that Town and Gown have always existed in harmony. They certainly have not. In the 1890s the two newspapers in Logan, one Democratic and one Republican, regularly analyzed the activities on the Hill in relation to their own viewpoints; and during World War I, the College was compelled to organize a Council of Defense to investigate the loyalties of foreign employees whom townspeople suspected of pro-German sympathies.

There has always been a community concern that the professors teach too liberally, but there was no real difficulty during either McCarthyism or the Vietnam War. Recently there has been an economic concern because the University expanded its housing and food service divisions, creating a degree of competition. But the University remains the single largest employer in Cache Valley, providing not only jobs for local townspeople but enhancing the economic life of northern Utah. Historically, friction between Town and Gown has been minimal. Logan becomes home to generation after generation of students, and the city responds with warmth.

An aerial photograph of Logan and the campus of Utah
State University in June 1970.

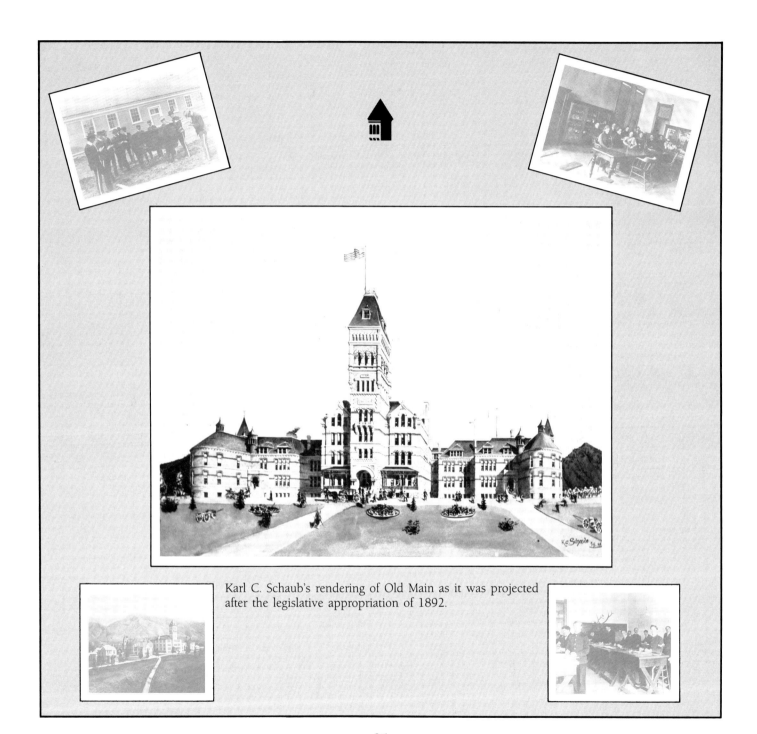

Karl C. Schaub's rendering of Old Main as it was projected after the legislative appropriation of 1892.

CHAPTER THREE

Old Main

President Stanford O. Cazier called it the "Flagship of the University." And it is. Old Main. The oldest building on campus, the oldest academic building still in use in the State of Utah, still the heart of the campus. A national historic landmark.

It was built piecemeal. In 1889, from the initial College appropriation of $25,000, the first Board of Trustees spent $20,528 building the south wing of a three-part structure designed by Salt Lake architect C. L. Thompson. It was in that lone south wing that instruction at the Agricultural College of Utah began on September 5, 1890, and it was in that lone south wing that instruction continued for the first three years.

It was not until 1892 that the territorial assembly appropriated money to finish the Thompson plans. The College had hoped for $60,000 for the biennium; but the assembly appropriated $108,000.

With that amount of money, the Trustees scrapped the Thompson plans that called for a final building of 100 by 270 feet and had the building redesigned by Carl C. Schaub. The new design was an enlarged structure measuring 190 by 342 feet, which the College catalogues between 1892 and 1904 described as "one of the largest college structures in the country."

The Thompson plans for the north and south wings were maintained, with only minor modifications. But whereas the Thompson plans called for a fairly compact central section joined directly to the wings, the Schaub plans called for a greatly enlarged central section and closed halls joining it with the wings.

One result of the expanded plan was to move the axis of the building seventy-two feet north from the center of the head of Fifth North Street. The original Thompson plan called for the tower to be due east of the end of Fifth North. But what was lost in the symmetry of the location was more than made up by the additional room—especially in the Main Auditorium.

There were some problems, however, with the Schaub plans. Although the building he projected was to be much larger than the Thompson Building, it would be so expensive that not even the generous appropriation for the 1892-93 biennium would cover it. So the Trustees made the decision to build the north wing and the east part of the central section and the enclosed halls that joined the central part to the wings. They would wait for another year to finish the front eighty feet of the building and the tower.

The enlarged building was completed for classes in the fall of 1893; but like the south wing, the building was built without electrical wiring. Not until 1895 were the floors ripped up and wires strung throughout the building. Until then kerosene lighted the structure and stoves provided heat in every room. There was no plumbing in Old Main until 1895, and even then the building was supplied from a brick-lined cistern east of the south wing, a cistern that

The south wing of Old Main, circa 1892. It was in this lone building that classes began in September 1890.

Right:
The Chapel on the first floor of the south wing in 1892. This was the Auditorium until the construction of the central part of the building. Daily chapel exercises were conducted and attendance was mandatory.

was fed by a pipe laid from the Logan, Hyde Park, and Smithfield Canal!

The Trustees had confidently assumed that the 1894 assembly would fund the completion of Old Main. But in 1893, with the demonitization of silver, the United States entered a prolonged economic depression. In 1894, the legislative assembly appropriated a meagre $15,000 to support the College.

Left:
The student body posed south of Old Main in the fall of 1893. Note the conservatory near the south tower—not completely removed until the construction of separate greenhouse facilities in 1909.

The physics lecture room in 1893. With the addition of a map, it was also the American history lecture room.

The School of Domestic Science taught its classes in Old Main until 1909.

Sewing classes were taught on the second floor of the south wing. This photo was taken in 1893.

Essentially, the entire College was housed in Old Main. The Library occupied one of the curved-front rooms in the north wing, and directly above it was the museum. The south side of the third floor of the center section housed the Chemistry Department. The Department of Domestic Science squeezed into the classrooms on the east side of the south wing (for sewing) and into the basement of the north wing (for cooking). Sharing the north basement was the woodshop, and, after 1895, the boiler room that supplied the building with steam heat and drove the equipment that ran the lathes in the shop and the separators in the creamery. The President's Office was tucked on the west side of the first floor of the south wing.

In 1893 the woodshop occupied most of the basement in the north wing.

The engine room in the basement of the north wing, 1893. Belts running from the engine turned woodworking equipment, the dairy equipment, and other mechanical gear in Old Main.

Even with its blank west front (waiting for the money to build the tower), Old Main was an imposing structure; and in the absence of trees on campus (the first were not planted until 1895), the building dominated the eastern half of the city of Logan. It was a perfect place for sending signals, and for at least fifteen years after 1894, that is how the roof of the south wing was used. In that year the College was linked to the Signal Corps by a direct telegraphic wire, and a flag system was devised to relay weather forecasts received from the War Department.

The *College Report* of 1894 described the service:

> The College receives the telegraphic weather forecasts from the forecast official of the Department of Agriculture located at San Francisco. The forecasts are telegraphed each day (Sundays and holidays excepted) at government expense. The signal flags are displayed from the flagpole of the College in full view of the valley below. These forecasts or warnings are of great value to the farming community. In 1893 the percentage of verification of the forecasts for the Pacific Coast division was 83.7.

In the absence of any student center, Old Main also served as the hub for student activities. The gymnasium that occupied the entire third floor of the north wing was built as much to provide a place for College dances as it was for a site for physical education and military science. Soon after the turn of the century, the first on-campus cafeteria was opened in the basement of the central section of the building. With a true eye to economy, the cafeteria was made part of the instruction in the cooking classes, and the coeds ran it under the direction of Domestic Science faculty members.

Not until 1901 did Utah's finances stabilize to the point that the legislature resumed appropriations for construction on the College campus. In that year, it appropriated $57,000 to the College. The bulk of those funds was directed toward completing Old Main – the west eighty feet of the central section and the tower, the high point, physically and aesthetically, of the building.

The gymnasium on the third floor of the north wing, circa 1895. It was in this portion of the building where the fire of December 19, 1983, started.

The west front under construction in the spring of 1902.

Though the Trustees still had on hand the Thompson plans from 1889 and the Schaub plans from 1893, they decided to advertise for new plans for the tower. The award went to H. H. Mahler of Salt Lake City. The Mahler plans called for a much less prominent tower than had either of the two previous plans. Schaub, in particular, had planned a massive tower rising some fifty feet higher than the one finally built. And it was Mahler's design that was built in 1901-2.

Building the final part of Old Main, including the tower in 1901.

Two views of Old Main showing the west front before and after the construction of the tower.

Things had changed considerably at the College and in Cache Valley between the time the south wing was built in 1889 and the tower was finished in 1902. The south wing had been built almost wholly out of locally produced materials. The sandstone water tables and other stone in the north and south wings, for instance, had come from Hyde Park; the stone for the foundation from the same Green Canyon quarry that provided the stone for the Temple and Tabernacle; and the brick had been burnt in Logan brickyards. For the last part of the building, most of the material came from outside of Cache Valley. Even the contractors, Bowman, Hodder & Company, were from Salt Lake. The massive red sandstone slabs that formed the front steps under the tower were quarried not at Hyde Park, but at Heber City, and shipped to Logan on railroad cars.

When the building was finished and opened for the fall term in 1902, there was another shuffle of departments and offices. The President's Office was moved to its present location, and the School of Commerce occupied the third floor of the tower wing. The Library was moved to the north side of the second floor, and other shifts of space and function occurred.

With the building's completion, the inevitable embellishment and remodeling began. A bell was hung in the tower the year it was completed. In 1909 the first senior class gift was an "A" placed on the west side of the tower (later carried to all four sides) and the classes of 1914 and 1915 installed a set of hand-played chimes, not replaced until 1978 with the installation of the Frances Winton Champ Carillon.

The Main Auditorium became the scene for plays and operas and concerts, a function not completely ended by the 1980s. After the Library moved into its own building in 1931, the vacated space became "The Little Theatre," home to the drama and speech departments for thirty years. In the middle of the 1970s, the center stairways were enclosed and an elevator installed. A stairway was installed beneath the Main Tower.

And, of course, the classwork continued. As the College expanded to the Quad, became Utah State University, and then expanded again far beyond the Quad, and even as the administrative offices naturally grew with the institution, Old Main remained at least partially a classroom facility. Even as the University marks its Centennial, scores of classes every week are taught in Old Main; and it is unlikely that a student can attend USU for four years without taking at least one class in this oldest of campus structures.

Right:
Champ Hall on the main floor of the central section, looking eastward toward the Auditorium, circa 1907.

Looking up Fifth North to College Hill, circa 1905, showing the recently completed tower.

On December 19, 1983, a fire gutted the north wing of Old Main.

Shortly before noon on December 19, 1983, an over-heated ballast in a fluorescent light on the third floor of the north wing started a fire in the old lath above the plaster. This was the area that had once housed the gymnasium, lined with tongue-and-groove redwood planking.

Fire gutted most of the third floor of the north wing, burning off part of the roof. Fire damage was held to a minimum by the prompt action of the Logan, Smithfield, and Hyrum fire departments, assisted by crews from the University; but the water that was poured into the building proved especially destructive. Thousands of gallons a minute were put on the fire for several hours.

Old Main restoration. Interior cupola support framing.

Old Main restoration. New steel beam support. Note charring to crossbeams.

Old Main restoration. Installing new roof sheathing prior to re-shingling.

The decision, of course, was to rebuild, and to rebuild the north wing as it had originally been built. During the Christmas break, the entire roof and third floor of the wing were removed. In succeeding months, the north wing was gutted, one of the three thicknesses of brick that comprised the walls was removed, and a new wall of reinforced gunite concrete was built within the old outer brick walls. The room layout was modified, but the discovery of curving bits of old woodwork above the false ceilings enabled the milling of new woodwork that matched the originals installed in 1893. Columns were run from the basement to support the new roof beams, which carefully duplicated the lines of the old roof; and an elaborate turret – removed after the earthquake of August 1962 – was rebuilt and placed on its original brick plinth.

The wing was completely rewired and replumbed and finished for use by the late fall of 1985, as was the second floor of the west wing, also severely damaged by the water and completely remodeled.

On June 3, 1970, in recognition of its state and regional role, Old Main was formally listed on the National Register of Historic Sites. At age one hundred, it continues to provide the symbol for the University.

The first aerial photo of the campus was taken in the spring of 1924 to use as advertising for the National Summer Schools.

CHAPTER FOUR

Feast, Famine, and Feast

The huge territorial appropriation of 1892 was the last for a long time. The Panic of 1893 cut deeply into territorial revenues, and in 1894 only $15,000 was appropriated to the College, as opposed to $108,000 only two years before. Classes were cut, salaries were cut, and every economy was exercised to even keep the doors open. But in 1894, the Agricultural College graduated its first class. Only four students received the baccalaureate degree, but eleven others received certificates in the commercial, domestic science, or agricultural courses. The next month President Sanborn resigned to return to his home in New Hampshire. He had come to organize the Experiment Station. He had become President and served during the crucial first years of the College's development.

He was succeeded by Joshua H. Paul, President of the Brigham Young College in downtown Logan. Paul's administration of only two years was marked by the effective beginnings of the Extension Service when the Experiment Station obtained money to hold a "Farmer's Encampment" in each county in Utah—bringing the research work of the College to its rural constituency. Paul was President in 1895 when the state constitution was written, fixing the position of the Agricultural College as a constitutional item; but Paul was also an avid Democrat and used his position to advance his party. It was a situation that was bound to offend half of the new state of Utah. And it did. Paul was dismissed by the Trustees and was succeeded at the Agricultural Col-

lege by his predecessor at the Brigham Young College, Joseph Marion Tanner.

A polygamist, President Tanner moved out of the President's House and into a downtown residence. The President's House became a women's dorm. Tanner successfully lobbied for funds with the new state legislature that allowed an expansion of the curriculum and the construction of the Mechanic Arts Building and a conservatory for the Botany Department. He also insisted upon requiring advanced degrees for new members of the faculty and upon increasing admission and graduation requirements.

Ultimately, however, it was his much-married status that raised enough opposition to President Tanner that, like his predecessor, he was asked by the Board to resign and did so in 1900. As they had with Paul and Tanner, the Trustees chose a President of the Brigham Young College, William Jasper Kerr, to be the College's fourth President.

Kerr was an aggressive leader who had a broad vision of what the College could become. He reorganized the faculty (for the first time providing faculty ranks) and regrouped the various departments into separate schools of Agriculture, Engineering, Domestic Arts, Commerce, Manual Training, and General Science. A School of Music was added in 1903. That same year, a summer school was added specifically to allow teachers in the area to pursue both baccalaureate and advanced degrees, and in 1903 the first master's degree was conferred.

The Agricultural College of Utah campus in the spring of 1899. The first trees were planted the previous year. Note that the tower and front of Old Main had not been built.

The third President (1896-1900), Joseph Tanner, in the President's Office in the south wing of Old Main.

The Mechanic Arts Building, built in 1897, was the first instructional building on campus other than Old Main. It was funded with an appropriation from the state legislature.

William J. Kerr, fourth President of the Agricultural College of Utah, 1900-1907.

The Mechanic Arts Building was gutted by fire on September 11, 1905, and partially reconstructed the same year. The fire destroyed many of the early records of the College.

The expansion of the curriculum brought an expanded College. Enrollment climbed from 380 in 1900 to 733 in 1904. In the same time the faculty increased from thirty-three to sixty. Inevitably, Kerr's aggressive leadership made enemies, especially John A. Widstoe, the Director of the Experiment Station, who felt that agricultural studies were being sacrificed to the expansion of other fields of study.

Widstoe resigned, joined the faculty of Brigham Young University, induced several of his ACU colleagues to join him, and used the pages of the *Utah Farmer* to attack Kerr and the Agricultural College. There were other, more serious attacks— perhaps not unrelated to the first. Governor Cutler suggested that there were serious duplications between the College in Logan and the University in Salt Lake City and that some restrictions on curricula should be mandated. Other interests introduced a bill to amend the state constitution to consolidate the College and the University of Utah. By heroic efforts Kerr and his allies in the state senate defeated the second proposal, but on March 20, 1905 the Governor signed a bill restricting the courses offered at the Agricultural College and forbidding it to offer courses in "engineering, liberal arts, pedagogy, or the profession of law or medicine." The act gutted much of Kerr's efforts to expand the curriculum. Nor was that the only threat. In 1907 a second bill to consolidate the College and the University barely failed in the state legislature.

Yet until the battles with Widstoe and with the legislature, Kerr had succeeded admirably. In 1901 funds were secured to complete the tower wing of Old Main. When the Mechanic Arts Building burned in 1905, it was rebuilt in an enlarged form, and new buildings were added to the Experiment Station facilities. Kerr also secured an important appropriation for regional dry-farm studies around the state. However, Kerr's resignation had been requested by a Board that had included the mother-in-law of John A. Widstoe—who was appointed as Kerr's successor in 1907.

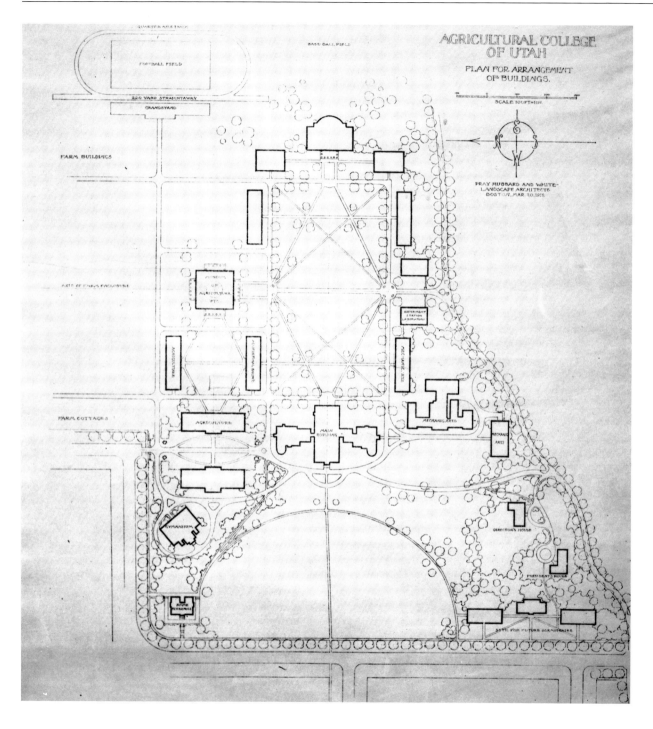

Facing page:
The master plan of 1912 has governed subsequent University growth.

The Hubbard, Pray & White rendering that corresponds to their 1912 master plan.

John Andreas Widtsoe, fifth President of the Agricultural College of Utah, 1907-16.

Elmer George Peterson, President of Utah State Agricultural College, 1916-45.

Widstoe rigidly adhered to the reduced curricula mandated by the legislature (although the state did allow a School of Agricultural Engineering in 1911) and went so far as to sign a formal treaty with the University of Utah in 1914.

Yet, having acceded to the legislature's mandates, Widstoe lobbied effectively for the state to adequately support the programs that were left. Mechanic Arts was expanded; the Chemistry Building was built (later named for him); an Extension Division was added, and the first county Extension agents in the United States employed and sent into the field; the Smart Gymnasium was built (largely from private funds); and significant increases in faculty and staff salaries were secured. Since it was evident that the institution would survive, a master plan was drawn in 1912 by a firm of Boston landscape architects— though the named buildings proposed for the campus still rigidly adhered to the legislative restrictions.

When Widstoe resigned in 1916 he was succeeded by E. G. Peterson, thirty-four-year-old Director of the Extension Service who was to serve as President for the next twenty- nine years. Peterson had graduated from the College and had served on the faculty during the Kerr administration. He shared Kerr's dreams for the College and Widstoe's for the Experiment Station and Extension Service.

Peterson's administration was immediately tested by the American entry into World War I; but President Peterson and Governor Bamberger were able to turn it to advantage. The campus became a military training camp, and the War Department allocated funds for the construction of barracks. The Governor persuaded the Federal Government to turn the money over to the state for the construction of permanent buildings that might be used after the war for the College, guaranteeing that the state would make up any necessary difference. The War Department complied; and in the winter of 1918-19 the Engineering and Plant

A historical pageant was held to commemorate the Quarter-Centennial of the College.

The northeast section of the campus, circa 1916, from the roof of Smart Gymnasium.

World War I appropriations funded the Plant Science and Ray B. West buildings, here shown under construction in February 1919.

Science buildings were built around the area that in 1912 the landscape architects had outlined as The Quad. The 1917 legislature had approved funds for the Animal Science Building, and the three buildings were built in quick succession, almost doubling the size of the College in two years. With the new buildings, there would never again be any question of consolidating the College with the University of Utah. Utah State had room for the future.

The campus was leveled and replanted in the early 1920s. Here a tractor breaks up the ground on the Quad.

The Quad was developed in the 1920s, following plans drawn in 1912. This photo, circa 1924, shows the tent city erected every summer on the site of the present Merrill Library to house the farmers and homemakers encampment.

The barns and corrals of the Utah Agricultural Experiment Station were key parts of the campus until the 1950s. This view from the 1930s shows the roof of the fieldhouse in the distance.

The Quad was planted to grass and landscaped, and the three new buildings were all in use by the fall of 1920. There was more than enough room for all the classes offered by the College, and the upper floors of the new Plant Science Building were used as living quarters for married students, the first married student housing provided by a college or university in the country.

The Family Life Building, constructed in 1935, was one of four structures built with federal assistance during the Great Depression.

In 1938 USAC marked its Semi-Centennial. The cornerstone of Old Main was opened on March 8, 1938, fifty years after the College was chartered.

The new facilities enabled President Peterson to convince the Governor and legislature in 1921 to allow classes in education to be taught at Utah State. That was a major breakthrough, and to capitalize on it, in 1924 Peterson scraped together every available cent and sponsored a National Summer School, drawing some of the greatest scholars in the country to Utah State as special faculty, and comfortably housing them in the married student rooms in the Plant Science Building. Summer school enrollment jumped

from 471 the previous year to 1,377 drawn from twenty-three states and five foreign countries. The National Summer Schools in 1925 and 1926 were equally successful, so successful that in 1927 the legislature virtually repealed the restrictive act of 1905, liberating the allowable curriculum at Utah State.

The Great Depression hit the College as it did every other factor of American life. Faculty members accepted cuts in salary and worked for promissory notes for part of the salary that did remain. In part, because of this commitment to teaching and students, enrollment did not really flag during the depression. In addition, the various work programs that were funded by the state and federal governments helped support students. The National Youth Administration provided work for some 2,000 of our students between 1934 and 1936, including a major employment program to gather and preserve the artifacts and the history of the institution for its Semi-Centennial in 1938.

But taken together, the progress in the 1920s and 1930s was spectacular. Although new instructional buildings were not immediately necessary, some peripheral construction was done. A Home Management House was built in

An aerial photo of Utah State Agricultural College at the beginning of World War II.

1927–essentially completing the plan of use for the President's House when it was built in 1891 as a model farmhouse. The Stadium was also built on campus, with Governor George H. Dern turning a very modern first shovel–by using a steam shovel. The Library was started in 1930 and federal projects built the Family Life Building in 1935, the fieldhouse, and Lund Hall, built as a women's dormitory (and the first dorm on campus since 1909) in 1937. The concrete amphitheatre was built as another federal project in the 1930s, replacing a wooden one on the site. In 1936 the new College of Forestry moved into the old Domestic Arts Building (previously the Boarding House)

after the completion of the Family Life Building to house the Home Economics School.

In addition to the expansion of the curriculum and the physical facilities, a major event was the accreditation of the Utah State Agricultural College in November 1926. Classes at Utah State were thereafter assumed to be on an educational par with every other accredited college and university in the United States.

With the entry of the United States into World War II, major expansion of the College stopped for the duration, and when the war ended in 1945, so did the tenure of E.G. Peterson, after twenty-nine years as President.

The corps of cadets parades before Old Main, circa 1907.

CHAPTER FIVE

In the Service of the Republic

The Land-Grant Act of 1862 and its various amendments in the succeeding years specified that military science and tactics would be one of the subjects taught at Land-Grant Colleges. The acts also specified that the War Department would provide the necessary instructors and equipment for the instruction. But the War Department did not move without considerable prompting. During 1890 and 1891 President Sanborn tried, without success, to secure a military science program for the newly established Agricultural College of Utah.

He was finally successful in 1892 with the arrival of Lt. Henry D. Styer of the United States Army. Styer's appointment was marked by the Board of Trustees with the creation of the Military Department and by making military science compulsory for all students. The catalogue noted:

> The marked advantages of this practice to young men has led several colleges to extend the privileges of military drill to young women with the most happy results. The spear, light rifle or some other light weapon is usually carried. The young women of this college are required to take military drill unless excused by request of their parents.

The Logan *Journal* also commented on what one wag called the "AC Amazons": "The main feature of the Military Department of the Agricultural College will be the Female Cadets. They will uniform and drill according to regulation tactics."

In the absence of any sort of physical education program at the College, the required drill for both sexes was made part of the curriculum; but there must have been considerable resistance, for in 1893 compulsory drill for women students was dropped in favor of a more genteel kind of P.E. taught by Miss Clare Kenyon and called "Physical Culture."

From 1892 to 1955 military science was compulsory for male students at the College. The War Department provided a stand of rifles in 1892 and eventually threw in a surplus Civil War cannon to augment the cadet corps' complement of arms. A room in Old Main was set aside as an armory– initially in the basement of the south wing and later on the third floor of the north wing near the gymnasium. The annual Military Ball became one of the highlights of the College's social season; and photographs of the student body during the 1890s and the early years of the twentieth century are marked with cadets proudly wearing the blue and gold of the United States Army.

But, at least initially, more than just the students were affected by the military science program. A fading photograph from 1902 shows Lt. Samuel W. Dunning drilling a group of paunchy faculty members on the stage of the Chapel in the south wing of Old Main–an auxiliary to the corps of cadets.

Whatever the skills the cadets learned in their program at the Agricultural College, they were soon called into play.

The corps of cadets and the College band parade on the stage of the Chapel, south wing of Old Main, circa 1894.

For a few years in the early 1890s, women students were enrolled in military drill. They marched and practiced with lances and wooden rifles.

Bugles blow as a drill instructor checks a cadet's rifle on the lawn southwest of Old Main, circa 1902.

A proud part of the armory of the Agricultural College of Utah cadets was this field piece – Civil War surplus.

An orchestra of World War I doughboys poses in the basement of Old Main, 1918.

During World War I, the College was virtually closed and its facilities used for military training. A barracks occupied the main floor of the Smart Gymnasium.

In 1898 ACU students volunteered for service in the Spanish-American War where their first instructor, Lt. Styer, won some fame in the Philippines; and in 1916 ACU cadets were among those in a "Motorcycle Reconnaissance Unit" sent to the Mexican border in pursuit of Pancho Villa.

With the entry of the United States into World War I in April 1917, the facilities of most of the Land-Grant institutions were pressed into service in the national interest. An ROTC program to train officers for the American Expeditionary Force was established at the College, and in 1918 the War Department ordered the establishment of a basic training post at the College to train those who intended to enlist in the army. Thus was born the Student Army Training Corps, the SATC. (Some in downtown Logan joked that the initials stood for "Safe At the College.")

The Corps took over most of the campus buildings. Main Auditorium and the Smart Gymnasium became barracks. Mechanic Arts was commandeered for officers' quarters; and specialized courses for radio operators and motorpool repairmen were taught in spare corners of the buildings. The Extension Service was mobilized to provide

A group of trainees on the Quad, 1918. The trees at right are the first forest plots planted at Utah Agricultural College—now the site of the Library and the Business Building.

During World War I, a major part of the activity of the College through its Experiment Station and Extension Service was to encourage the production of food. Here Old Main Hill is ploughed for "Victory Gardens" in the spring of 1918.

The 145th Field Artillery, having been trained at the College, was demobilized on campus on February 18, 1919. Old Main was decorated with the flags of the victorious Allied nations (the U.S., Great Britain, France, and Belgium).

Below:

Red Cross volunteers at the Logan depot met troops disembarking from OSL trains in February 1919 for the demobilization of the 145th Field Artillery. At the time, the Spanish Influenza epidemic was raging in Europe and the United States. Note the "flu masks."

as much information as possible on growing food to the residents of the state of Utah, and Old Main Hill was ploughed as a Victory Garden.

Of course, the College also did the usual silly things that the United States does in time of war. A Council of Defense investigated the loyalties of all Swiss and German employees, asked for reasons why people failed to subscribe to the "Liberty Loan" bond sales, and checked out the rumors that a professor in the Animal Science Department was really a half-brother of Kaiser Wilhelm II!

With the armistice on November 11, 1918, the troops returned to Logan to be discharged. The soldiers paraded down Main Street in Logan, and Old Main was decorated with the flags of the victorious Allied nations. But the victory and the demobilization were marred by the outbreak of the Influenza epidemic of 1918-19. Troops were quarantined in Old Main, flu masks became standard gear for soldiers and civilians, alike, and men who never saw the trenches of the Argonne were buried in the Logan City Cemetery within sight of the College.

In the 1930s women re-joined the USAC corps of cadets.

Sam Brown Belts and all, the ROTC corps of cadets parades on the Quad in the early 1930s.

With the return of peace, the ROTC program continued; and it was continued on a campus that the war had changed forever. Monies appropriated by the War Department for housing the troops were used by the state of Utah to begin an Engineering Building and a Plant Science Building. This increased the College's instructional space by one-third and began to outline the Quad where the ROTC cadets drilled during the 1920s and 1930s—in the 1930s again joined by a women's program, the first since 1893.

World War II brought new military activity to the USAC; but it is activity that it is difficult to document in a photographic history. Whereas World War I activity at the College is fully, even monotonously documented, very few photographs on the defense activities at the College during World War II survive outside of the National Archives. The rigid security that marked much of American life was certainly felt in the photographic record of the College, part and parcel of a nation that got accustomed to posters advising that "Loose Lips Sink Ships."

From 1892 to 1954 military training was required of all male students at the College. This color guard parades in the 1940s when three-year students were mobilized for overseas service.

During World War II the College offered an array of specialized training courses for defense industries, as this float from the Hyrum, Utah, Fourth of July parade in 1941 advertises.

Army (including air corps), navy, and marine detachments were trained in communications at the College, monopolizing the Field House and Mechanic Arts Building and bunking in out-of-the-way corners in Old Main where ashtrays were, for the first time in the building's history, "officially" present and where "stimulants" were not unknown.

While specialized course work was being conducted, the ROTC program was accelerated. Three-year students were immediately sent off for final training and then abroad to one of the thousand places that the United States garrisoned or guarded or contested during four years of war that ringed the globe. So scarce were males at the College that in 1943 the traditional Valentine's Preference Ball chose a "Most Preferred Coed" rather than a "Most Preferred Man." Most dances were suspended for the duration. What was the song the country was singing? "They're Either Too Young Or Too Old!"

Carrier planes were based and carrier pilots trained on fields at USAC during World War II.

An Army Air Corps training plane flies above Benson, northwest of the campus, during World War II.

"Rosie the Riveter" was also a fixture on the USAC campus during World War II.

The war brought the air force to campus—at least the navy air arm, and the planes that ultimately led to the addition of aerospace studies to the military science program. Carrier pilots were trained at the College, at the Logan-Cache Airport, and at an airstrip northeast of the campus, where the airstrip simulated a carrier deck and ended at the brow of the bench—it was fly or else on that strip.

Other parts of the College were also brought into play during the war. A small garrison housed at the Campus guarded German and Italian prisoners of war captured in the North African campaign. Sent to Utah because the Geneva Convention specified that POWs must be sent to a climate similar to the one from where they were captured, the prisoners were used as supplementary farm workers in labor-short Cache Valley. The Extension Service again helped mobilize the forces for a larger food supply, the College of Education undertook work at the Topaz Internment Camp in central Utah (a fine service for the College, but a scar on the moral fibre of the Republic).

The corps of cadets on parade on the Quad, 1950.

After the war the ROTC program was renewed, and its graduates – and other College students – saw service in Korea and Vietnam. Aerospace studies joined military science in offering programs at the University, programs that were broadly supported. In 1947 more second lieutenants were commissioned from Utah State than from any other school in the country with the single exception of the U. S. Military Academy at West Point. That crop of "j.g.s" earned Utah State the nickname: "West Point of the West." However, after the dropping of compulsory ROTC for all men, enrollment decreased dramatically. The Thursday-at-noon tradition of drilling on the Quad disappeared and the cadets are much less obvious to contemporary students.

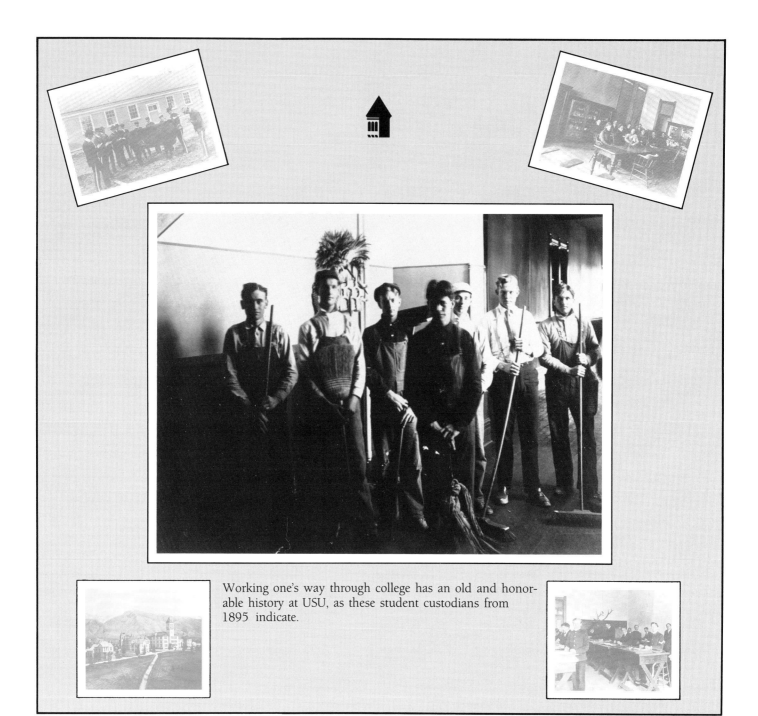

Working one's way through college has an old and honorable history at USU, as these student custodians from 1895 indicate.

CHAPTER SIX

Student Life

Utah State University exists for teaching, service, and research; and its students come to Logan or study at one of the regional University centers to learn. But there is a life beyond the library and the classroom and the laboratory and the late-night studies at the dorm desk. There is a society beyond and around those constants of University life.

In the early years of the College's history, it was a much constricted society, paternalistic and Victorian. Although the Lund Act forbade sectarian influence, the founders of Utah State University were products of the nineteenth century's Evangelical Christianity. Significantly, the auditorium in the south wing of Old Main was called "The Chapel."

When the College opened on September 5, 1890, the rules governing student behavior contained a requirement for daily attendance at the 8:00 A.M. chapel exercises. These rules further stated that "these exercises will be wholly devotional and completely non-sectarian. They are conducted by the Faculty and in part by members of each of the churches represented in Logan."

The rules further required that each student under the age of twenty-one attend church services on Sunday. Stepping into parental shoes, the rules explained:

When students do not bring a request [from home] to be excused from church attendance it is assumed that the parents desire the faculty to enforce their wishes in this respect. This assumption is made because it is

known that parents generally desire that their children attend church.

President Sanborn, a devout Methodist, had very clear views on such things. He also had very clear views on the Sabbath. He revised the College's schedule so that classes were held from Tuesday through Saturday with a holiday on Sunday and Monday. It was a schedule that lasted until World War I and was imposed because of the President's assumption that students would always rest on the first day of a holiday and study on the second—and Jeremiah Wilson Sanborn wanted to make sure that the day they rested was a Sunday!

But chapel exercises continued. In 1916 they were changed to a weekly schedule, and so they remained, gradually evolving into the lyceum programs and student assemblies that met in the Main Auditorium every Thursday morning at 10:00 A.M., an hour that was completely unscheduled for classes. The Thursday Assemblies lasted until 1963, when the growth of the student body created a demand for the Thursday morning time slot for new classes.

Even with close supervision, some students did escape. There exists in University Archives a fascinating exchange of correspondence from 1895 between President Joshua H. Paul and downtown Logan saloonkeeper J. R. Edwards. The President wanted Edwards to keep college students out of his Main Street watering hole. Edwards refused. Paul

Daily chapel exercises in the south wing of Old Main, circa 1891. The balcony was later removed and a second floor was added to house the Geology Department.

The women's reception room in the dormitory was the scene of sedate courting in the 1890s.

A long way from the present Student Health Center, this photo shows the house at the bottom of Old Main Hill that was used as a quarantine hospital by students in the early days of the twentieth century.

drove downtown in his buggy to do his own investigation; and the two men got in a fight, first in the saloon and then on the boardwalk. Edwards was fined for assault and battery. Five dollars.

With the President and the faculty keeping such a close eye on the students, it is not surprising that much of student society revolved around the College and its programs. The institution's first dozen years saw the organization of several clubs and societies that provided a major social outlet for students. The Longfellow Literary Society specialized in recitations and book reviews and in writing and reading their own poetry. The Periwig Club introduced the drama at the College years in advance of any formal theatre classes in the curriculum. Some organizations were purely social, like the AC Women's Club, still functioning at the University's Centennial.

Of course, many of the organizations were short lived and were very much geared to particular classes or particular instructors. Lt. Robert J. Binford put together a rifle team from members of the cadet corps. During the winter of 1914, when he could find nowhere else for his men to practice,

he set up a target range in the third-floor hall of Old Main, with his sharpshooters at the south end of the building and the targets—and lots of sandbags—in the gymnasium at the north end. Needless to say, the practice resulted in a furious round of letters from President John A. Widstoe.

Raising the flag at the Moses Thatcher home in downtown Logan after it was acquired as the first home of Sigma Chi.

A Glee Club from the 1930s.

Before the construction of dormitories during the 1950s, the College acquired downtown houses for use by students. The David Eccles home became a dorm for upper-class women in 1946. In 1956 it became Kerr Hall, a dorm for forty-five men students.

USAC's first Chi Omega Sorority House.

Local fraternities and sororities, initially organized as dining and residence cooperatives, started with the formation of Sorosis, a women's club, on January 24, 1898. In 1934 it became the Beta Xi chapter of Alpha Chi Omega. Local fraternities like Phi Delta Nu in 1903 and Pi Zeta Pi in 1905 also later affiliated with national fraternities. While there have been fluctuations in local establishments, by 1986 there were three national sororities and seven fraternities represented on the USU campus.

Some clubs did not have an easy time. The local Intercollegiate Knights tried to organize as early as 1912, but President Widstoe grandly announced that there would "be no club." Undeterred, they organized anyway as — what else — the "Benos."

Lund Hall, built as a WPA project in 1937, was the first dormitory on campus since 1908.

Although student life has always been centered on the campus, for most of the institution's history, the campus provided no facilities for housing the student body. The College Boarding House, a co-ed dorm, opened in 1891, but closed in 1909 and was remodeled to become the home for the School of Domestic Science. From then until the construction of the Stadium Apartments and Lund Hall in 1937, students were expected to board downtown in private apartments. The transportation problem was solved in 1912 when the tracks of the Logan Rapid Transit Company were extended to the campus. Indeed, it was the desire for an on-campus residence that led to the formation of the first fraternities. Although various facilities were at times devoted to student housing, it was not until the 1950s with the construction of several dorms for both men and women students that the majority of the student body lived on the USU campus.

There was one exception. The building of the Plant

The top two floors of the Plant Industry Building, constructed in 1917-18, were used to provide the first married student housing.

Married students outline their class year.

Surplus army barracks were moved to the campus after World War II and used for married student housing, the "University Apartments," until 1967.

Industry and Education Buildings (Ray B. West Building) after World War I gave the College more space than it could conveniently use. Consequently, the upper floors of Plant Industry were remodeled into a series of apartments for married students—the first married student housing in the country to be provided by an institution. During the National Summer Schools of the early 1920s, visiting faculty members were housed free in those apartments in Plant Industry—housing that allowed the College to be competitive for the visiting scholars.

With the end of World War II and the rapid growth of the College with married veterans returning to school, a series of Quonset huts, trailers, and army barracks formed a village east of the campus for married students. Some of those dorms, colorfully known as "the Lambing Sheds" for the number of young children who lived there, remained until the 1960s when the construction of the new University Apartments (the Triads) was completed.

Parking is no new consideration on the Utah State University campus. This wintertime photo from 1902 shows sleighs and buggies parked on the present site of the Taggart Student Center.

With dormitory construction in the 1950s and 1960s, USU became a residential campus; and the problems of a residential campus accordingly emerged as a consideration for campus planning. Parking—a problem even in the early days when students' horses were stabled during classes in the Model Barn—became a constant factor in planning, and a sure source of indignant letters to the editor of the campus paper. As the Experiment Station barns and test plots were moved from the campus to locations out of Logan, much of the cleared space formerly occupied by them was paved for new lots.

Clean-up day on the Quad, 1909.

Students reading an issue of *Student Life* (now *The Statesman*), probably waiting in registration lines on the second floor of the south wing of Old Main in 1907.

And the residential campus also saw a change in the composition of the student body. From the first foreign students who enrolled at the Agricultural College of Utah in 1911, by 1985 over one in ten of the resident student body were foreign students from fifty or so countries around the world.

Just as so many organizations and professional associations began with informal student effort, so did the first on- campus publications. In November 1902, the first issue of *Student Life* was published. Then a quarterly magazine, it was first issued in tabloid format in 1908. The name was changed to *The Statesman* in 1978; but the paper, the oldest continuously issued student publication in Utah, is still printed on a tri-weekly basis.

The first literary magazine, *Agi-Literose*, had equally informal student beginnings, eventually becoming *Scribble* and later *Crucible*. The Junior Class began publishing a yearbook, *The Buzzer*, in 1908, a publication that continued until 1971.

The student-body organization began in 1907. Today, the Student Senate has charge of a substantial budget, and student representatives sit on all major University policy boards. Things were more informal in the beginning. One of the early student governments even passed a resolution directing that anyone who did not show proper enthusiasm at the Pep Rally before the annual game with the University of Utah was to be thrown into the Logan, Hyde Park, and Smithfield Canal.

Although students have always been the key reason for the University's existence, for much of the institution's history, they were also key players in its operation. An annual clean- up day involved the entire student body and faculty in the manual labor necessary to maintain the institution. Agathon, for years a spring celebration, was marked with the construction of new sidewalks around the campus, sidewalks built by the students, themselves. Many a brass or marble plaque still sits in walks around campus indicating that the walk dates from "A-Day" in a particular year.

Foreign students have long played an important role in both fieldwork and scholarship.

This photograph from the 1960s shows students from Iran with President Daryl Chase.

On A-Day in 1919, students installed a sidewalk along the north side of the Quad.

Aggie fans cheer from the bleachers during a football game at Adams Field in the 1920s.

Freshman beanies (white for girls and blue for boys) were required until 1964.

Right:
Campaign posters are a springtime constant on the USU campus. These signs are from the 1926 campaign.

The Senior Circus was an opportunity for organized craziness, as this photo from March 20, 1915 shows.

The Military Ball, attended by the Governor and First Lady of Utah, was the highlight of the social season. This Ball from the 1920s was held in Smart Gymnasium.

Dancing in the 1950s.

The Aggiettes, 1956.

As befitted an institution that until 1957 was known as the "Agricultural College," the coed milking contest was a major event in the 1920s.

The Winter Festival with a snow sculpture contest was a major event when the snow was ample—as it usually is on the USU campus.

Whatever it is, it looks fun, circa 1923.

The cast of the operetta *Iolanthe* posed on the stage of Logan's Capitol Theatre, February 16, 1925.

Before computerization, registration was held in the field-house, more crowded then than for basketball games.

Grand Opera *(Aida)* was sometimes presented on the stage of the Old Main Auditorium.

As the University reaches its Centennial, the Taggart Student Center is the hub of student activity; but for most of the University's history, no such facility existed. Not until the construction of the Family Life Building as a WPA project in 1935 was there even a facility for informal gathering. After World War II, one of the many surplus army barracks erected on the campus was christened the Temporary Union Building, the TUB, and served as the student center until 1952 when the first section of a new Union Building was erected where the animal husbandry barns and corrals had once stood. The UB provided a spacious ballroom, cafeteria, bowling alley, bookstore, game room, and study areas. There have been two major additions to the facility and it now houses most of student services as well.

"The Bird" was the source of endless coffee, discussions, and cigarettes. When this photograph was taken in 1946, the only other place to smoke was at "Nicotine Point" above the amphitheatre.

In 1935 the cafeteria moved from the basement of Old Main to the basement of the Family Life Building, where this photograph was taken.

The Snack Bar in the Temporary Union Building (the TUB) in 1947. The building was in use from about 1946 to 1952, when the present University Center was completed.

An aerial view of the Utah State Agricultural College campus in 1952, just at the start of the institution's growth. The Union Building (now the Taggart Student Center), still under construction in this photo, is in the center.

CHAPTER SEVEN

From College to University

The war ended and President Peterson retired in 1945. It was a time of dramatic change. Franklin S. Harris, President of the Brigham Young University, became the seventh President of what by then was called the Utah State Agricultural College, the USAC.

With the demobilization of the United States Army and the liberal benefits guaranteed by the GI Bill, enrollment at USAC skyrocketed. In 1943-44 the institution enrolled fewer than a thousand students. In 1946-47, that figure had climbed to 4,493, an increase that strained both the College's and Logan's capacity to deal with it. Many of the students were returning soldiers with families. They needed special housing. Barracks, Quonset huts, and trailers were pressed into service.

Surplus army and CCC barracks were moved to campus where, during the late 1940s, half the classes were being taught in such buildings. Inevitably, the buildings were labeled as "temporary." Equally inevitable, some are still in use forty years later.

President Harris left in 1950, to be succeeded by Louis L. Madsen. Madsen was an agriculture professor with great knowledge of federal programs and practices. It was not an easy time. The growth of the institution had long ago left the College's initial constituency in a small minority when compared to later curricular and research growth. A cut in state appropriations and an aggressive Board of

Trustees who were determined to hold expenditures to a minimum created many problems in the day-to-day administration of the College. And Madsen was caught in the center of all those conflicting demands. Governor J. Bracken Lee fired Madsen in 1953. Madsen was succeeded by Henry Aldous Dixon who, in turn, shortly resigned to run for Congress.

In 1954, after nine years of upheaval, Daryl Chase became the College's tenth President. Three years later, on Founder's Day, 1957, Governor George Dewey Clyde (former Dean of the School of Engineering at USAC) signed an act of the state legislature changing the name from Utah State Agricultural College to Utah State University.

The change from College to University was a process— and the official name change was a mid-point in that process. From a primary emphasis on technically oriented undergraduate education in 1940, by 1965 Utah State's commitments to graduate education and research were major in virtually every academic area.

The institution's first master's degree was awarded in 1903, growing to the thirty-one conferred at the 1933 commencement. Throughout the 1930s and early 1940s various departments and schools established graduate curricula, leading in 1945 to the formal organization of the School of Graduate Studies. The next year Utah State inaugurated courses leading to the doctoral degree. As the University

Franklin Stewart Harris, President of USAC from 1945 to 1950, began the institution's foreign contracts and welcomed its first major group of foreign students.

In this aerial photograph from the summer of 1946, the central campus is still dominated by the buildings and test plots of the Agricultural Experiment Station.

Immediately after World War II, enrollment climbed from 950 to 4000. Many students were returning servicemen and women with families. The College housed them in Quonset huts, trailers, and decommissioned barracks that formed a new city east of the campus.

With mushrooming enrollment in the late 1940s, classes were crowded into makeshift facilities.

marks its Centennial, master's and specialist's degrees are conferred in some sixty fields of study and doctorates in two-thirds that number.

Enrollment mushroomed as the national economy remained strong after the end of World War II. From an enrollment of 3,858 in 1954 enrollment soared to 12,000

The chimes in Old Main were rung manually in the early 1950s. Eighth President Louis L. Madsen looks on.

Henry Aldous Dixon, ninth President of USAC, 1953-54.

by 1986. And the physical plant of the University expanded commensurately. In the late 1950s, new buildings were built to house the Colleges of Agriculture and Natural Resources (then called Forest, Range, and Wildlife Science). The decision was also made to provide on-campus dormitories for part of the student body. Four women's dorms and two for men were built from the proceeds of a special bond issue, the bonds to be retired from housing charges.

Daryl Chase was President of USU from 1954 to 1968.

Governor George Dewey Clyde, former faculty member and Dean of Engineering, signs the act of the Utah legislature changing the name of the institution from Utah State Agricultural College to Utah State University, March 8, 1957.

Above:
This photograph from the summer of 1952 shows the beginning of the perennial parking problem at USU. In the background at left, the first floor of the Union Building is under construction.

Left:
In the early 1950s a single "computing machine" occupied a room in the basement of Old Main. At the University's Centennial, Computer Services is a major unit and virtually every office on campus has at least one computer.

It was in the 1950s that the campus moved dramatically and finally beyond the confines of the Quad. The growth of the University occurred against a background of relocating the on-campus Agricultural Experiment Station animal research facilities to off-campus facilities.

The Agricultural Science Building, constructed in 1955-56, was the first major construction on campus for purely academic or research purposes since the Family Life Building in 1935.

Below:

Literal center of the campus as well as of campus activities, the Union Building (now the Taggart Student Center) was built in 1952-53. This 1965 photo shows the 1964 addition. Another addition was dedicated in 1987.

Owing to the dramatic growth of USU's student body in the 1960s, the campus was expanded for student housing. This aerial photo shows the Triads (University Apartments) and the LDS Living Center, later acquired by the University for additional single-student housing.

The Natural Resources Building was constructed in 1960. Two years later the entrance was embellished with the largest mosaic in the Intermountain West, designed and executed by Professors Everett C. Thorpe and Gaell Lindstrom of the USU Art Department.

The construction of the High Rise Dormitories in the mid-1960s continued the policy of housing a large percentage of the total student body on campus.

The Eccles Business Building, dedicated in 1970, is the home of the College of Business and is the tallest building in Cache Valley. USU has the oldest business school west of the Mississippi.

Dr. Glen Laird Taggart, President of Utah State University from 1968 to 1979.

The enormous spurt in construction in the mid-1960s occasioned by a public facilities building bond authorized by the Utah State Legislature changed the physical appearance of the campus every year from 1965 to 1980, with considerable attention being paid to the replacement of the so-called "temporary" facilities. In 1954 the entire physical plant of the College was valued at $8.1 million. Fourteen years later, in 1968, the physical plant was valued at $62 million in authorized and funded construction.

The campus from which President Chase retired in 1968 was dramatically different from the one to which he had come as President in 1954. Succeeding him was Dr. Glen L. Taggart, a Cache Valley native with extensive experience in Land- Grant College administration. Although much of the program of the Taggart years represented a consolidation of past gains and a straightened budgetary situation because of national and international recessions, the College's research growth took an enormous leap. In

An aerial photograph of the Utah State University campus in
the summer of 1970, by Ted Hansen.

As the University grew and new buildings were constructed, old ones were demolished and replaced. In the fall of 1970 wrecking crews leveled the University Annex. Built in 1891 as a dormitory, it became the first home of the College of Family Life in 1909. It was later used by the College of Natural Resources and subsequently by departments in the College of Humanities, Arts, and Social Sciences.

Right:
The University Inn, constructed in 1980, provides a campus residence for visiting researchers and scholars who participate in the University's Life Span Learning program.

1954, research expenditures (largely by the Experiment Station) totaled some $1.4 million. By 1978, over $18 million from all sources, public and private, were spent in research programs that circled the globe and stretched above it. The graduate program grew to the point that by the approach of the Centennial, over one student in five was in some sort of advanced-degree program. International programs were intensified and the Land-Grant Mission expanded.

A key part of the growth has been the development of off-campus centers for University instruction, with Logan faculty flying or driving to various parts of the state to offer classes. The flights to Moab and Roosevelt became legendary. One of Glen Taggart's crowning achievements was a Kellogg Foundation grant, which allowed for the construction of a University Inn directly east of the Student Center. Utilizing private funds, the grant was matched and another building which provides meeting space for special conference visitors, was erected southeast of the Inn. On campus, this Kellogg Life Span Learning complex has arranged a conference center and living quarters for short course or seminar participants from around the United States and abroad. The Extension Service has been consolidated with the campus and with the Life Span Learning programs.

Stanford Cazier, President of Utah State University since 1979.

Stanford Cazier, a former USU history professor, returned to Utah State University in 1979. Administering during a time of severe state budgetary restraints and decreased federal spending, Cazier has utilized a combination of donated private sources, student fees, and state monies to expand the campus. In this Centennial year, under his administration, several major building projects have been undertaken, and the Research Park was created to transmit research into commercial use for the people. Some alumni such as the Eccles family have assisted in the construction of the Business Building, Life Span Learning facility, Museum of Art, and a new education building. The University continues to provide the necessary facilities for a tremendous educational experience.

The Nora Eccles Harrison Museum of Art, constructed in 1984.

Facing page:
Aerial view of the central campus in 1987, on the eve of the Centennial.

The baseball team of 1903 posed in a downtown Logan studio for this shot. The team's manager was also the President's private secretary, John L. Coburn.

CHAPTER EIGHT

Aggieland

When the Agricultural College of Utah opened for its second year in the fall of 1891, a few students and several members of the faculty organized some intramural scrimmages on the rocky wasteland east of Old Main, a wasteland that later became the Quad. Some professors, trained at eastern colleges or at the University of Utah where football was haphazardly played, had seen the game played before. A few may have actually played it. With that sort of local expertise and a couple of well-thumbed rule books, football was launched at the College.

The lack of organization was matched by the lack of interest shown by Town and Gown alike. None of President Sanborn's letters mentions athletics, and the two Logan newspapers, *The Journal* and *The Nation*, ignored it.

The next year saw a change in both the President and the press. President Sanborn's son Harry was chosen team captain, and *The Journal* covered the first intercollegiate game played at the College, a Thanksgiving Day match with the University of Utah. Whoever was the reporter, his words represented quite a beginning for athletics at the institution:

> The great football game has been played. The Agricultural College boys met the University students and the latter are the former's.
>
> In this city there is no disappointment over the result – i.e., after the University people had departed.
>
> The score stood twelve for the Agriculturalists and nothing for anybody else.

> The University team wore brown pants, white jumpers, red stockings and a smile of confidence.
>
> The home team wore clothing to protect them from the weather. In other words, they dressed as each man pleased.
>
> Back and forth the two teams surged and the excitement grew apace. Blood flowed, mud splashed and hearts fluttered.
>
> To an unsophisticated spectator it might have been taken for a rough and tumble fight.
>
> Finally the game ended and the score was announced with many cheers for the victorious students of the Agricultural College.

There is no record of any sort of intercollegiate activity for 1893; but the Logan paper noted that "the physical culture of the boys and girls falls to Lieutenant Styer in the armory and Miss Kenyon in the gymnasium." After compulsory drill, it is likely that the cadets had little spare enthusiasm for sports.

Such sports as there were were purely voluntary and had a ready mix of students and faculty. Team captain from 1894 until 1900 was Willard Langton, first as student and then as instructor. The same situation held in baseball. Not until 1901 was the faculty barred from participating in college games, games which were organized in a very informal way. The first full-time coach and Physical Education instructor was Dick Richards, employed in 1901.

The College's first athletic field was constructed in the first years of this century east of Old Main on a rocky field that later became the Quad. Note the track banked with lumber in this 1905 photograph.

The 1901 football team was the first in the University's history to train under a full-time coach. It was also the first team to be confined solely to students. Earlier teams had comprised both students and faculty—and anyone else who showed up for the game.

Until 1913 football games were played on the field east of Old Main. It was the responsibility of the players to pick the rocks off the playing field before matches. This photo shows a practice play in 1907. Standing at rear is Captain Edgar B. Brossard, later Chairman of the U.S. Tariff Commission.

Though women were required to drill as part of the ROTC program in the early 1890s, by 1903 women students were taking part in a more genteel sort of physical education called "Physical Culture." This photo from 1902 shows an early form of aerobics—with dumbbells and coordinated footwork—in the first gymnasium, on the third floor of the north wing of Old Main.

The Aggie basketball team of 1904. Note the padded knickers and the stockings. Games were played in the College gymnasium on the third floor of Old Main.

Richards brought a full scope of athletic training to the College, a scope limited by the institution's gymnasium, which comprised the entire third floor of the north wing of Old Main. Below regulation size, it was not really adequate for anything but exercise classes. Behind the building, in what is now the Quad, the first track was laid out in the late 1890s, and in 1904 a banked track was made of two-by-eights from the local lumberyard. But it was these beginnings that gave birth to both the school colors and the school nickname. On November 7, 1901, a special meeting of the faculty adopted Royal Blue and White as the College colors. The name Aggie had a more informal beginning, with the first teams called "The Farmers." Aggies, a contraction of Agriculturalists, was first used in the late 1890s though as early as 1916 the *Journal* called the various athletic teams "Big Blue"—an apparent reference to the Blue Ox of Paul Bunyan stories.

The third-floor gymnasium was shared by men and women students; and it was in that third-floor gymnasium that apparently the first intercollegiate basketball game was played in 1903—by an ACU women's team against a team from the Brigham Young College in downtown Logan.

An intercollegiate track meet on the old field east of Old Main, circa 1905. The track ran due north-south from a point near the present Maeser Labs to the parking lot east of the Education (now Ray B. West) Building.

But there were real drawbacks to the gymnasium in Old Main, not the least of which was the fact that the men's dressing room was in the basement of the south wing. That meant a run the length of the building and up three flights of stairs to reach the gym. And, even though the gym uniforms of the early twentieth century were hardly scanty, the sight of bare male arms and bare male knees alarmed some. Miss Charlotte Kyle, instructoress in English, wrote a letter to President Widstoe protesting the scantily clad athletes in Old Main. The President agreed, and promptly appointed Miss Kyle to raise money for a proper gymnasium! She obtained $10,000 from Trustee Thomas Smart, and with additional funds from the state, the Smart Gymnasium was built in 1912.

From 1912 to 1971 Smart Gymnasium was the home of Aggie athletics and physical education, dominating the north end of Old Main Hill. The building was condemned after the earthquake of August, 1962, and demolished in 1971.

The west end of the Quad hosted baseball games and tennis matches in the 1920s.

From 1913 to 1927 football games and track meets were held on Adams Field below the campus—the east half of Adams Park.

The next year, 1913, the College acquired its first athletic field: half of Adams Park on Fifth North and Fifth East below College Hill. For the next thirteen years, that was the home of the College's track, football, and baseball. In 1918, E. L. "Dick" Romney became the Athletic Director and Head Coach of all major sports. And it was at Adams Park that the games were played in the first conference to which the College belonged, the Rocky Mountain Faculty Athletic Conference (RMAC). The College won the first conference championship in football in 1921, and five years later Governor George H. Dern broke ground for a stadium on campus—using a steam shovel!

On October 12, 1926, Utah Governor George H. Dern broke ground for Romney Stadium on the UAC campus. A thoroughly modern event, the Governor broke ground with a steam shovel!

In 1938, the building of a new fieldhouse (identical to that built at the University of Utah) gave the College its first adequate basketball court for intercollegiate play, and essentially completed the physical education and athletic facilities for the succeeding thirty years.

Because it is located in the Rocky Mountains, on a former shoreline of Lake Bonneville, Utah State University offers a prime setting for winter sports. Until the 1970s beginning ski classes and intramural competitions were held on College Hill below Old Main. This photo was taken in the 1940s.

By 1932, Romney had a staff of six and the College fielded teams in most of the major intercollegiate sports, including swimming, tennis, and wrestling. During the 1930s, Romney was tremendously successful and brought numerous championships to the Aggie campus. In addition, a full range of intramural sports were played on the campus. With membership in the major Intermountain athletic conference, the Aggies had come far from the days when its athletic schedule included meets with teams from Salt Lake City high schools, Fort Douglas, and even the State School for the Deaf.

Archery and fencing have been taught since the early years of this century.

Though offered as a physical education class only in recent years, Utah State University did field an intercollegiate golfing team in the 1950s and 1960s. These students practice their swing on Old Main Hill.

Students have always been involved in intramural and personal physical education classes at Utah State. Bowling classes have been taught since alleys were added to the Taggart Student Center facility in 1952.

Left:
Women have long participated in both intramural and intercollegiate sports events.

Intramural football occupies the Quad each fall. This photo is from the 1950s.

Foreign students, first from the Middle East and more recently from Latin America, introduced and popularized soccer on the USU campus.

Pep rallies, complete with bonfires, were a staple of home football games from the 1890s to the 1970s.

Until May 1961, USU continued as a member of the conference, later known as the Skyline Conference. In that year the conference was reorganized, and USU was left outside of it as an independent – a situation that lasted until 1977 when USU formally joined the Pacific Coast Athletic Association. Aggie football and basketball reached new heights during the 1960s. A new recruiting emphasis combined local and outside talent to the degree that USU football teams went to bowl games in 1960 and 1961 and Merlin Olsen was awarded the Outland Trophy as America's best collegiate lineman. The 1959-60 basketball team won twenty-four of twenty-nine games and featured a top-ten ranking and a National Invitational Tournament berth. Numerous NCAA post-season berths followed, but tragedy struck the campus when Wayne Estes, an All-American and USU's first East-West All-Star, was accidentally electrocuted following a game during his senior year, 1965. In 1970, the Aggie basketball team came within one game of going to the national finals.

Merlin Olsen, USU football star in the 1960s.

Wayne Estes, one of USU's All-American basketball stars.

It was during that time that a major effort was made to upgrade the athletic and physical education facilities on the campus. The upgrading became crucial after the Cache Valley earthquake of August 1962 resulted in the condemnation of most of the facilities in the Smart Gymnasium. The pool in the gym had to be closed after chunks of concrete falling from the ceiling interrupted a swim meet.

A new special events center that would accommodate basketball games and other events needing upwards of 10,000 seats, the Spectrum, was built by 1970-71 as was a new football stadium that initially seated 20,000 fans. A new building to house Health, Physical Education, and Recreation was completed in 1971 on the site of the old Romney Stadium. A special track stadium, named for long-time track coach Ralph Maughan, was built near the new Romney Stadium, giving the University a major athletic complex stretching over five city blocks. The Nelson Fieldhouse was remodeled and featured an indoor track and tennis and basketball courts.

Discus champion L. Jay Sylvester attended USU from 1956 to 1959 and later went on to compete in the Olympic Games in 1964, 1968, 1972, and 1976.

Physical education is much more than field and court events. Testing, training, and development also play a part. Dale O. Nelson of the HPER faculty tests Rod Tueller in this photograph from the 1950s.

Track and Field events have been staged in four places on and around the campus. This photo from the 1950s shows a hurdles meet in old Romney Stadium. In 1968, the Ralph Maughan track was dedicated.

Amid the expansion, the occasional NCAA play-off berths, the televised events, and the considerable institutional pride and prestige that were involved, there were controversies. One of the greatest centered not on the teams or the players or the coaches, but on the attempt in 1969 to change the nickname of the team from Aggie to Scotsman. A furious campaign finally resulted in the retention of the name Aggie, but a gradual downplaying of it in favor of the less occupationally direct Big Blue.

Athletics has become a gigantic business for universities. With potential television revenues, the economic payoffs are extremely significant. During the 1970s women's sports also received national attention as universities were required to offer a women's program. Although national championships were achieved in volleyball and softball, it has been difficult to maintain superior programs. The costs for scholarships, recruiting, travel, and staff significantly stretch a limited budget. However, alumni and students are most anxious for athletic success because it is an important part of USU's heritage and can create memories of a positive campus experience.

NEW STADIUM FOR UTAH STATE UNIVERSITY, LOGAN, UTAH   G. EUGENE HATCOCK & ASSOCIATES - ARCHITE

Romney Stadium was built in the mid-1960s on the northwest corner of the USU campus. It is the fourth location
where Aggie football has been played.

A biology class held in Old Main, circa 1902.

CHAPTER NINE

Classrooms and Laboratories

It is too easy to see the history of an institution like Utah State University in terms of the superlatives of its external existence: size of budget or faculty or buildings or student-body enrollment or books added to the library. But it is in the classroom and in the laboratory that the institution's prime mission occurs—the interaction between teacher and student. Great teachers leave their mark in broadened outlook and increased expectations. And it is just this central part of the University's reason for existence that is invisible. Only the backdrop of the rooms can be measured.

When the Agricultural College of Utah began instruction on September 5, 1890, the physical plant of the College consisted of the south wing of Old Main, a few houses, the Model Barn, and the Experiment Station Building. The south wing contained only six classrooms; and while the regular college enrollment was not large, the high school students in the Preparatory Department swelled the total enrollment to nearly 250.

From the institution's first days, some classes have been taught in what was essentially a laboratory situation. Some of the first animal husbandry courses were actually offered in the Model Barn; and the President's House was built as a laboratory school for the School of Domestic Science (until President Sanborn moved in and moved Domestic Science back to Old Main). But most instruction was carried on in rooms at the new Agricultural College of Utah that varied little from the rooms in which the students had been taught in the public schools of the territory. A bare classroom with desks and blackboard became a history class with the addition of a map, or a room for chemistry or physics with the addition of a periodic table of the elements. Instruction was very much a case of lecture, reading, and recitation. Regardless of the space problems inherent in a growing institution, the first Presidents of the University—Sanborn, Paul, Tanner, and Kerr—saw that space largely in terms of four walls enclosing sufficient desks and chairs.

But the Morrill Act provided for the teaching of the "mechanic arts" in the Land-Grant Colleges. That phrase implied a very hands-on experience; and as the physical plant of the institution grew, so did its instructional space and the opportunities for varieties of instruction. The construction of the north and center parts of Old Main in the years between 1892 and 1902 enlarged the number of laboratories and classrooms, including some that were purposely designed for vocational or technical instruction. The Dairy Building near the north wing (and driven from the same engine that provided power to the woodshop) was a key lab area in instructing students in the manufacture of cheese and butter (and some of those students were later to play an important role in the development of the Cache Valley dairy industry). The Mechanic Arts Building of 1897 was entirely comprised of areas for vocational instruction.

The University campus, itself, has been the outdoor laboratory for surveying since the opening of the University in

1890. This class, wearing the uniforms of the corps of cadets, surveys the Old Main Hill in 1895.

By 1893 the University had acquired enough instructional material to establish its own museum on the third floor of Old Main, above the Auditorium. Space was still at enough of a premium that the Student Army Training Corps stacked their rifles adjacent to the geology display.

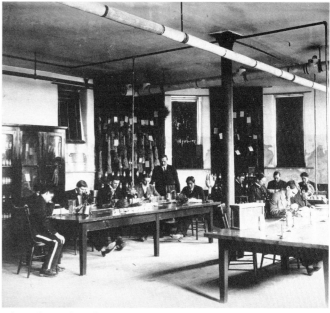

This plant identification class, circa 1896, met in the basement of the south wing of Old Main.

A class in laundering met in the basement of the north wing of Old Main in 1902.

This clothing and textiles class, circa 1903, met in the Department of Domestic Science on the second floor of the south wing of Old Main.

The first announcement for classes in typing announced that students would learn to become "type-writers." Later usage confined that term to the machine. This class met in Old Main, circa 1902.

The Dairy Building, circa 1903, was constructed east of the north wing of Old Main. It was one of the first instructional buildings on campus.

As the curriculum expanded and became more sophisticated, so did the need for specialized quarters for the various areas of study. For instance, the temporary chemistry laboratories on the third floor of Old Main clearly created some problems, since they were located next door to the business classrooms. There were other problems. President Widstoe complained to the Chemistry Department that the students were throwing out of the windows chemicals that were eroding the mortar between the bricks. He had a similar complaint about the art students dumping paint pots that were streaking the walls with purples and golds and reds.

The chemistry laboratory on the third floor of Old Main, circa 1900. The loss of ceiling plaster in the upper left may be the result of faulty plastering, or of a faulty experiment.

The original courses of instruction at the College had been firmly fixed, with little opportunity for students to sample many studies beyond those that were prescribed for their degrees. In 1913 that changed with the wholesale remodeling of graduation requirements and the allowance for a substantial number of elective courses. While that liberalization of the curriculum allowed for a fuller education of the students, it also meant an expanded curriculum and, consequently, a greater crush in the limited space available on campus.

It was not until 1916, with the completion of Widstoe Hall specifically for the teaching of chemistry, physics and bacteriology (one of the first courses in the country), that

Below:

The Library reading room on the second floor of the tower wing of Old Main, circa 1905. Since the Library reading room was the largest on campus with tables, banquets were often held there. After the Library moved to its own building in 1931, the area became the Little Theatre.

specialized labs were given their own quarters in a building that was adequate for their use. It started a trend that has continued to this day. Old Main was a building full of rooms that would answer almost any function to which they were put. Buildings since Widstoe Hall have been purposely designed for the specialized uses planned for them, with the exceptions of the Plant Science and West buildings, which were built by the War Department as barracks.

The Animal Science Building was built in 1917, again for a specific use, as was the Family Life Building in 1935 and the Library in 1930. Before 1930 the Library occupied any place that was available. It started on the first floor of the south wing and was moved in 1893 to the north wing, and then to the second floor of the tower wing, directly over the President's Office. Not until 1930 was a space specifically designed for a modern library operation—well-enough designed, in fact, that the 1930 Library is still in use, incorporated in the west front of the Merrill Library built in 1963.

The College Bank, circa 1907, was a hands-on practice bank for the School of Commerce.

The Agricultural College of Utah was one of the first institutions of higher education in the United States to offer business courses leading to a bachelor's degree. This photograph of a class in the School of Commerce dates from 1909.

Though built for the scientists employed by the Utah Agricultural Experiment Station, in the 1890s the station's labs—in a building between Old Main and the President's House—were sometimes used as laboratories for classes at the College.

The Library in the 1940s. Though constructed in 1930 specifically for Library purposes, the building also housed the English Department, which was moved from the north wing of Old Main when the Library was completed.

Class changes in the first years had been announced by a handbell rung on the hour by the President's Secretary. After the completion of the Old Main Tower in 1902, a bell large enough to sound over the entire campus was installed and it regularly rang the hours until the various buildings were wired with electric bells. Just as well. With the huge growth beginning in the 1960s, the campus would have outgrown even the bell in Old Main Tower.

In 1969 the total area of all buildings on campus was two million square feet. By 1985 that figure had doubled. And the uses were increasingly specialized. In 1890, the largest single expense that the Trustees had to face in completing the south wing of Old Main for the opening of school was the purchase of chairs and desks. Nearly a century later, some buildings contain specialized equipment and instruments worth many times the cost of the structure that houses them.

Dr. Milton R. Merrill, long-time Vice President for Academic Affairs at Utah State, taught his political science classes in Old Main, circa 1956.

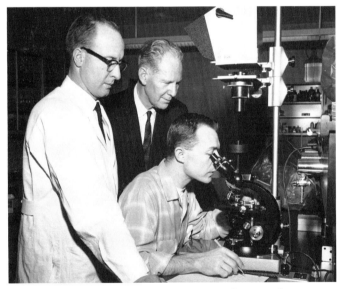

Seminars are taught in small rooms across the campus. These photos, circa 1965, are of the Joel Ricks Seminar Room in Old Main (top) and the Hatch Room (bottom), an Elizabethan room installed in the Library in 1953.

Research classes demand increasingly sophisticated equipment. Dr. John Simmons and Dean Eldon Gardner conduct a biology lab in the 1960s.

The bacteriology lab in the Natural Resources Building in the 1960s. The first degree-granting program in bacteriology in the West was offered at Utah State University.

History Professor Blythe Ahlstrom in the 1960s using maps and photos to discuss the Spanish-American War.

Left:
A biology class in the 1960s.

The Agricultural
Science Building
in the 1960s.

Below:
In the 1960s the Language Laboratory was established to
provide taped exercises in grammar and pronunciation of
foreign languages.

It is the phenomenal growth of the research programs
that has both spurred new construction and altered its com-
plexity. In the ten years from 1968 to 1978, outside funding for University-conducted research rose from $2.8 million
to almost $18 million. Since 1978 it has more than tre-
bled again. New programs have accelerated the trend. Until
1959, almost all research on campus had to do with either
the literature available in the Library or other libraries, or
with agricultural and water engineering studies. In 1959,
the Electro-Dynamics Laboratory was established. The
Water Research Laboratory in 1965 and the Space Science
Laboratory and Center for Research in Aeronomy in 1969,
and since then the Ecology Center, the Space Measurements
Laboratory, and a dozen other specialized centers that
involve University staff and students are concentrated on
the home campus.

The Utah Water Research Laboratory at the mouth of Logan
Canyon was built in 1965, extending the on-campus
research facilities dramatically.

The Maeser Laboratories Building houses the Chemistry Department. It was built in 1968 on the site of the old Model Barn. This architect's drawing is from 1968.

It is a concentration that has drawn collaborative research programs from federal and state agencies, and now, with the development beginning in 1986 of the University Research Park, from private industry and business.

As it approaches its Centennial, Utah State University educates its 12,000 students in fewer than 100 classrooms and 50 laboratories that are centrally scheduled. Research facilities (including offices and seminar rooms) comprise the great majority of the total square feet on the USU campus.

Overall, the critical need for classrooms and research facilities will constitute as much a challenge in USU's second century as it did in its first.

A geology class outing in 1911.

CHAPTER TEN

The Campus Beyond the Campus

Though rightly centered on the home campus in Logan, the interests of Utah State University have historically stretched far beyond its institutional center. As part of the Land- Grant system – and as home to the Utah Agricultural Experiment Station – the University was founded with the idea that it would take its discoveries from the campus to the people. During the first year of operation (1890), the Experiment Station conducted thirty-six formal studies and published four bulletins, publications extensively quoted in the state's press.

In 1896 the first state legislature passed the Cazier Act, providing an appropriation for the Experiment Station to hold an annual Farmers' Institute in each of the new state's twenty-seven counties. It was the effective beginning of the Extension Service.

Since water is *the* key factor in all agriculture, all development, indeed, of all life in the arid West, it is understandable that the first major investigations of the Utah Agricultural Experiment Station dealt with water, or the lack of it. One of the first formal experiments dealt with dry-farming. It is still an active research subject for the Station.

In 1903 the state legislature authorized the establishment of six branch arid farms throughout the state to perfect dry-farm agriculture and to test the geographic limits of its applicability. Test results reported to the Station offices in Logan led to publications of bulletins and to Director (later President) John A. Widstoe's classic *Dry Farming*

(1910), scientific publications that effectively established the main parameters of dry-farming. Its perfection showed directly in production statistics. In 1907 Utah had 93,799 acres (mostly irrigated) planted to wheat. By 1915 there were more than 500,000 acres (mostly arid) planted to the same crop.

In 1911, the Experiment Station placed one of its employees, L. M. Winsor, in Vernal. Essentially the first county agent in the western United States, he was called to Washington to help launch a federally backed county agent and extension program under the Smith-Lever Act, becoming the first of many of the staff who have served the national government. By 1922 the Extension Service (formally organized at the College in 1906 and supported by federal help since 1913) had agents in all of the counties in Utah. Originally focusing on the educational needs of the farm population, over the years their duties and responsibilities have expanded to include the 4-H clubs throughout the state and specialized urban programs in the major population centers.

At the same time, the College expanded in a more traditional way. In 1913, by legislative decision, the Normal School at Cedar City became a branch agricultural college of ACU. In 1951 Snow College in Ephraim was also made a branch campus (both remained part of the institution until 1966); indeed in 1957, when the College became a University, its seal showed stars representing Logan, Cedar City, and Ephraim, and the motto, "The State is Our Campus." Very soon, that became literally true.

In 1967, after the Governor vetoed a proposal to establish a junior college in the Uintah Basin, Utah State University was charged with teaching college courses there, flying teachers from Logan to Roosevelt and Vernal. The Uintah Basin Center for Continuing Education provided the model for centers that were later established in southeast Utah and in the Sevier Valley. Programs sponsored by the Continuing Education Center and the Extension Class Division took USU faculty throughout the state and into southern Idaho.

Below:
The Greenville Farm in North Logan conducted the first scientific studies that measured the application of water to crops and vegetables, circa 1908.

In 1903 the state authorized the Experiment Station to open and operate branch farms around the state. This is the entrance to the St. George Experimental Farm, circa 1905.

In 1904, before county agents were located in the field, a lecture train furnished by the Union Pacific Railroad toured Utah and Idaho carrying exhibits from the Experiment Station.

The first major University expedition was the Natural History Field Expedition, which conducted studies in southern Utah in 1938.

Experiment Station farms and test plots are located in many parts of the state. Here, in 1956, President Daryl Chase and College of Agriculture Dean R.H. Walker visit the Farmington Farm.

The USAC Forestry Camp in Logan Canyon in 1936. A former CCC Camp, it serves as an off-campus laboratory facility for the College of Natural Resources.

The first radio broadcast from Cache Valley was from the farmers' encampment of 1925. President of the Board of Trustees A.W. Ivins is in the center, and College President E.G. Peterson is on the far right.

University programs had long played in various downtown Logan locations until 1960, when the University acquired the historic Lyric Theatre on Center Street. Completely restored to its Edwardian elegance, the theatre reopened with "Hamlet" on April 3, 1961.

The first USU radio station was KVSC, which went on the air in 1949. Later the University was the home of Channel 12, KUSU.

More than just faculty and classes, the University's voice has gone beyond the campus via radio and television—first from live or taped broadcasts from Salt Lake City stations and in 1949 with the University's own AM station, KVSC: later to become KUSU-FM, the state's oldest public radio station.

But beyond the formalized instruction offered by the branches and embodied in the work of the Continuing Education and Extension Service Centers, the University and its student body very early participated in major functions off the campus. In 1893 the Agricultural College of Utah won a bronze medal for its exhibit at the Columbian Exposition, the Chicago World's Fair. The College regularly exhibited at the Utah State Fair and at World's Fairs in St. Louis in 1904 (where it won a gold medal), at the Lewis

The Agricultural College of Utah began exhibiting at state fairs and at international expositions in 1893. This photo from the Utah State Fair in 1910 shows the display of dry-farm grains from the state experimental farms.

and Clark Exposition in Portland in 1905, and at the Panama-Pacific Exposition in San Francisco in 1915. Nor were the exhibits solely agricultural. The medal won at Portland was for an exhibit submitted by the Mathematics Department.

During the Great Depression and World War II, Utah State had been increasingly involved with federal and state planning. Experiment Station specialists had worked with the Land Resettlement Administration in agricultural lands surveys, reclamation, and new crop introduction. It was this accumulated expertise that prepared the University for its enlarged role in the post-war world.

Some Utah State faculty members moved to Iran in 1939 as advisors to the Iranian government on water, soils, and crop management. After the war and the inauguration of Franklin S. Harris as the College's seventh president, international involvement increased dramatically, with the institution administering President Truman's Point IV programs in Iran and participating in Greece, Turkey, and Lebanon. And foreign student enrollment followed the College's interest beyond the borders of the Republic.

This photo of the Chairman of the Board of Trustees and an Iranian farmer was taken in August 1954, during a formal visit to Iran by USAC officials to sign a long-term advisory contract with the Iranian government.

Throughout the 1950s and 1960s international contacts grew; but it remained for the administration of Dr. Glen L. Taggart, who became the eleventh President of the University in 1968 to greatly expand and formalize that involvement. Dr. Taggart came from an important career

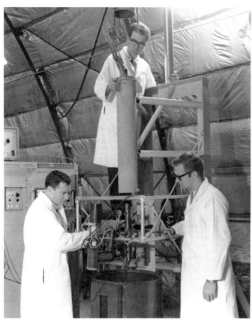

Aeronomy investigations at the University began the extension of institutional research beyond the campus–up!

Student experimenters on USU's "Get Away Special," the program that allows students to develop experiments to be sent up in the Space Shuttle.

as Dean of International Programs at Michigan State University. His experience and the University's prior experience came happily together.

While USU had participated in Peace Corps, Vista, and USAID projects before 1968, their impact upon the home campus was minimal. Some USU programs were staffed by outside people specifically employed to administer the programs. Under Dr. Taggart, the entire campus extended its involvement, with University personnel operating in foreign centers and then returning to the campus. International research and development projects also attracted students from a growing list of foreign countries where there was a USU presence. By 1987 Utah State University ranked third among U.S. universities overall and first on a per capita basis for its work in international development.

But the University's growing research involvement has also been extra-terrestrial. The Physics Department, the

Morton Thiokol's R. Gilbert Moore, an adjunct professor at Utah State University, bought the first "Get Away Special" payload from NASA and donated it to USU's Center for Atmospheric and Space Sciences.

The 120-acre Ronald V. Jensen Living Historical Farm is used as a laboratory for courses in experimental research, conservation, and living history interpretation.

A photograph of the Space Shuttle payload bay, which includes the USU Vehicle Charging and Potential (VCAP) experiment. This view of the payload bay and Earth was obtained on the seventh day of the Spacelab-2 mission, August 5, 1985.

Electro-Dynamics Laboratory, the Space Science Laboratory, and other campus research agencies have become increasingly involved in atmospheric researches. The first student-generated space project from Utah State was orbited on the Space Shuttle in 1982; and USU alumna Dr. Mary Cleave was a Shuttle crew member in 1985 – a crew member who carried a USU Centennial Banner on her multiple orbits. Continuing involvement led to the suggestion that the initials USU really stood for "Utah's Space University!"

Yet, with all the outreach of University teaching, research, and extension beyond the home campus, recent years have seen a return to one of the oldest forms of contact between USU and the larger community: bringing people to the campus for special programs. Brainchild of President Taggart and funded by the Eccles Family and the Kellogg Foundation, a continuing education complex was built in the very center of the campus in 1980-1981: the Life Span Learning Center that provides space for specialized conferences and course work and housing accommodations for participants. A long way from the tent city on the Quad of the 1920s.

But in looking to the future, the University has also looked to its past. The establishment of the Ronald V. Jen-

sen Living Historical Farm and the associated Man and His Bread Museum reaches back to the life that was lived and the life that Utah State University was initially chartered to address, to assist, and to augment. On a site six miles from the home campus, the farm life of many – if not most – of the University's first students and first patrons is re-created in the buildings, the equipment, and in the work of the students who study and re-enact those days.

From centers around the world, in space, in extension offices and experiment station sites, in branch campuses and continuing education centers, on a farmstead of the turn of the century, the University, its students, and its staff are involved. In 1956, S. George Ellsworth wrote of Cache Valley at the valley's Centennial of settlement, "The valley, like the living lake, has received and given fully in turn."

The same could be said of Utah State University.

Historic Old Main of Utah State University.

CHAPTER ELEVEN

Palimpsest

Utah State University is very much an institution living in the present and planning for the future. Yet its continuous life on the same site for the past century has made of the campus a record of that century, of that life that the photographs in this book seek to recall. It is not wholly a story of triumph, though there is triumph. There have also been trials. With production, there has been pettiness; with education and research there has been time-serving and sterility. But, overall, there has been progress—progress of a broad kind.

When Utah State University was chartered by the territorial assembly on March 8, 1888, it was essentially an agricultural high school. The first staff member employed was the Director of the Agricultural Experiment Station. Only later was the Director, Jeremiah Wilson Sanborn, also appointed as the first President of the Agricultural College of Utah.

Course work was practical and direct: agriculture, blacksmithing, home economics, yet the first book accessioned by the Library was *Philosophy: Historical and Critical* and in 1891 the College established a two-year business course, the first west of the Mississippi and one of the first in the Republic.

It was an institution founded in great hope, a hope that carried the first faculties through some very bad times. In 1893, the College suffered its worst budget cutback. The legislative appropriation shrank from $108,000 to $15,000.

Nevertheless, President Sanborn issued a positive statement about the school's ultimate success, "The vitality of the College is adequate to live through the biennial period before us, and it will proceed on its onward course with simply an abated speed." That represented a great deal of faith, and a great deal of truth.

Between 1894 and 1907 the College withstood three attempts to consolidate it with the University of Utah. In 1905 the curriculum was curtailed by state law.

Budget reductions.

Threats to its very existence.

Legislated limitation of its curriculum.

Yet, with all those pressures, in 1912 the College employed the Boston architectural firm of Pray Hubbard & White to develop a master plan for a University of 10,000 students with key planning elements being the development of the Quad and the localization of specific fields of study in different campus areas. Now, three-quarters of a century later—after vast campus expansion in physical plant, curriculum, and research interests since the 1960s—the University enters its second century with much the same sort of campus that was planned in 1912.

The campus is a palimpsest. Layers are there, layers of a century of students, of staff, of visitors—the purposeful and the merely curious.

One cannot walk across the Quad without walking with past lives: Presidents, scientists, leaders and the led. Beneath

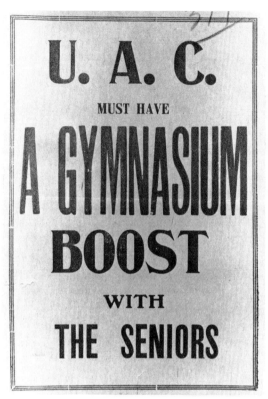

Handbill for the 1910 fundraising program for the Smart Gymnasium.

Even in 1901 there were "departmental" photos. This group is the English Department and Library staff.

the facade of the Merrill Library is the 1930 Library, and in a trap-door opening off the basement are the stumps of trees planted as the first forestry experiment in 1899 and whose branches shaded the Farmers and Homemakers Encampments of the 1920s. A grate in the parking lot east of the south wing of Old Main covers the cistern that—fed by a pipe from the Logan, Hyde Park and Smithfield Canal—supplied the University's first culinary water.

In his reminiscences, Fred Larsen recalled the campus in 1888, when the College was chartered:

"On Christmas morning 1888 Father, Chris and I climbed up the hill for a walk. We scared rabbits out along the rim. There was not a house on the whole flat where now the USU campus is located. Nothing but sagebrush."

Not until 1893 were the first trees planted on the campus and the rough turf and sage began to give way to lawns and landscaped grounds.

Around the campus there are plaques and markers and elaborate bas-reliefs that mark places and people and things that tie Utah State University to the life of the valley, the state, the region, the Republic, and the world. On the west steps of Old Main is a simple marker that reads "4778"—the level of Lake Bonneville, the Pleistocene inland sea, 12,000 years ago when the campus, itself, was created as a delta of the Logan River. Old Main, the Alumni House (formerly the President's House), and the Family Life Building, are all National Historic Sites, equivalent in formal listing and recognition to such places as Mount Vernon, the Statue of Liberty, and the White House.

Where the first scientific experiments on the application of water to crops and vegetables were conducted by the Experiment Station at the turn of the century, the first buildings of the University's new Research Park are rising.

The techniques may have changed since this photo from about 1901, but the problems of maintaining the plants and grounds of the University continue. It took two people to spray the fruit and ornamental trees on the campus eighty-seven years ago.

In 1900 the contributions the College could make to a country where most people lived on farms or in small towns were contributions to agriculture. Today, while contributions to agriculture and agribusiness continue, the spin-offs of other research are in the fields of high technology, and the acres that saw wooden sluices and measuring weirs now see Research Park businesses.

Married students live in apartments and mobile homes where navy pilots trained for World War II; and where veterans' families grew in the 1950s, the new Foods and Nutrition Building is the base for the most advanced research in food values.

In thousands of photographs; in millions of pieces of paper; in miles of audio, video, and computer tape housed in University Archives and in various campus offices is the record of the past. At every hand are the critical and the merely curious survivals of life on the USU campus for the past century, including the building specifications for Old Main that were used to help rebuild the north wing after the fire of December 19, 1983.

By 1909 when this Inspection Day photo was taken, the campus showed little of the landscaping that has since marked it. The building at left center is the Veterinary Hospital on the present site of the Plant Science Building.

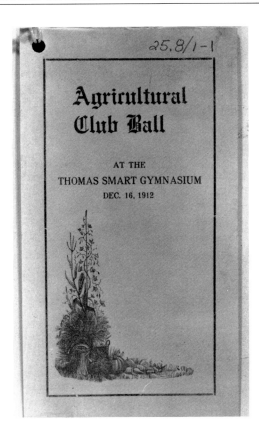

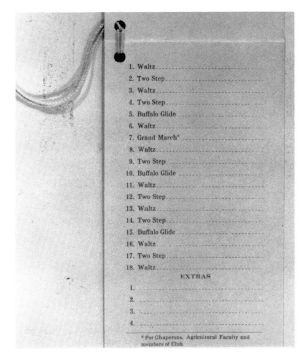

Above and Left:
Dance card for the Agricultural Club Ball, December 16, 1912.

It is to recapture another age to hold a dance card—complete with dangling pencil for entering partners—from, say, 1912, and see that the tango, introduced to the United States that very year by Vernon and Irene Castle, was also being danced in the newly built Smart Gymnasium, or to wonder just what the turkey trot or buffalo drag looked like on the floor.

The first University flag sits next to a special recognition awarded the University by the visiting national volleyball team from Japan in 1980. Off-campus or underground newspapers record past indignations and burning issues that everyone has now forgotten. Handbills plead for money to build a new gymnasium or protest censorship in the hanging of student art shows or urge a vote for a studentbody office.

Nearly a quarter of a million students have received some part of their education on the USU campus. For some, no doubt, it was a passing thing. For others, it was the watershed experience of their lives. New doors were opened, new careers chosen or old ones reinforced; sparks ignited in classes that led to lifelong interests and lifelong achievements, a quarter of a million pebbles in a pool where the ripples will take another hundred years to wash upon millions of shores.

The first "laboratories" on the campus were those for technical training. This blacksmithing class met in the Mechanic Arts Building in the 1930s.

Below:

The Family Life Building, a National Historic Site, was built as a WPA project in 1935. The original plans called for a fourth floor that was to be used as an art gallery. Funding problems eliminated the fourth floor, and it was not until construction of the Nora Eccles Harrison Museum of Art in 1984 that the University had an adequate museum facility.

Aerial view of campus, 1958.

Who can say where a powder-train lit so long ago by a teacher, or a book, or a conversation with friends, or perhaps only a sunset view over the trees on College Hill will lead? The University's students are stretched 'round the world; its interests now reach into the heavens beyond it. There are few fields of study in which USU students cannot wander, there are few springs of knowledge from which they cannot drink.

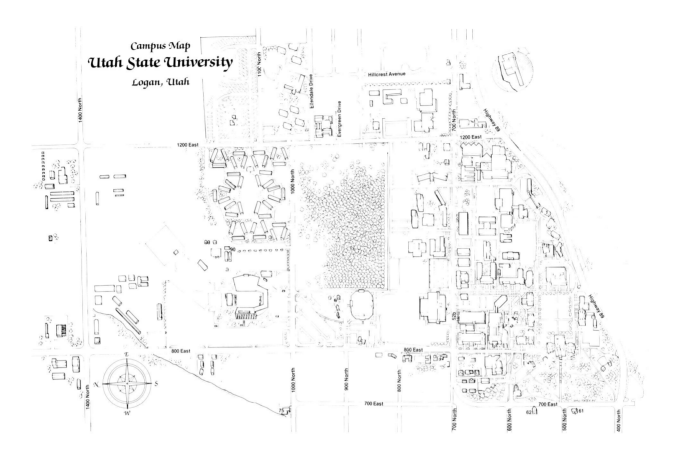

Utah State University campus map, 1987.

But at the University's Centennial, its staff and students, past and present, look not only to a present and a future so far beyond the imaginings of its founders, they look back a century – and rightly so – to the rude beginnings of this place upon a sagebrush hill, and can recall in thought, if not in mood, the lines to the first alma mater hymn of the Agricultural College of Utah, "How well I remember the days of 'Eighty-Nine.' "

Yes.

And much more.

Facing page:

How much history does each graduate walk past on the traditional commencement march each June? Here, looking from the tower of Old Main, is the graduation procession from 1965.

PRESIDENTS OF UTAH STATE UNIVERSITY

Jeremiah W. Sanborn	May 17, 1890 to May 31, 1894
Joshua H. Paul	June 1, 1894 to April 25, 1896
Joseph M. Tanner	April 28, 1896 to June 10, 1900
William J. Kerr	June 11, 1900 to March 26, 1907
John A. Widtsoe	March 27, 1907 to February 16, 1916
Elmer George Peterson	February 17, 1916 to June 30, 1945
Franklin Stewart Harris	July 1, 1945 to June 30, 1950
Louis Linden Madsen	July 1, 1950 to April 25, 1953
Henry Aldous Dixon	August 8, 1953 to December 3, 1954
Daryl Chase	December 3, 1954 to June 30, 1968
Glen L. Taggart	July 1, 1968 to June 15, 1979
Stanford Cazier	June 15, 1979 to

Book design and layout by Richard A. Firmage.

Editorial direction and production management by

Linda Speth and Nikki Naiser.

Typesetting by Type Center.

Printing by Publishers Press.

Binding by Mountain States Bindery.